Best Practices
from America's
Best Churches

Best Practices from America's Best Churches

Edited by
Paul Wilkes
Marty Minchin

PAULIST PRESS
New York • Mahwah, N.J.

Cover by Cynthia Dunne
Text design by Sharyn Banks & Cynthia Dunne

Library of Congress Cataloging-in-Publication Data

Best practices from America's best churches / edited by Paul Wilkes, Marty Minchin.
    p. cm
  ISBN 0-8091-4135-3 (alk. paper)
   1. Pastoral theology—United States—Congresses. I. Wilkes, Paul, 1938– II. Minchin, Marty.
BV4011.3 .B47 2003
253—dc21   2002156338

Published by Paulist Press
997 Macarthur Boulevard
Mahwah, New Jersey 07430

www.paulistpress.com

Printed and bound in the
United States of America

Table of Contents

CHURCH DYNAMICS:

MAKING MINISTRY WORK

ON THE EDGE:

RADICAL CHURCH MODELS

Introduction

A conference is often measured by the quality—and intensity—of the conversations that occur in the hallways after the workshops and presentations. If that barometer is used, the Pastoral Summit was an outstanding success.

The seven hundred Protestant and Catholic clergy, staff, and lay leaders who came to New Orleans in 2001 for this three-day gathering spilled out of workshop rooms and into the hallways of the Marriott Hotel in animated conversations. Although they already were people with a deep commitment to their local churches, what they were experiencing was truly unique: a gathering of some of the best practitioners from all parts of America, from all types and sizes of churches. The presenters at the Pastoral Summit were people who were blazing innovative trails in worshiping God, serving their people, reaching out to people beyond their walls, and making a profound impact on their communities.

After those workshops, those in attendance couldn't wait to get into the hallways to talk each other, and exchange stories and phone numbers. And, they continue to talk about those days in New Orleans. Informal Pastoral Summit networks quickly formed in cities and towns.

For those who were not in New Orleans, this book provides the Pastoral Summit experience. It is designed to assist those who continually seek new ways to reach and serve an increasingly complex and diverse group of spiritual seekers—the American people.

For churches are no longer what they were a generation, even ten years, ago. No longer can a Catholic upbringing or denominational affiliation be counted on to bring people to church. Peer pressure, some vague sense of duty—or guilt—have receded into the background of America's collective religious consciousness. Rather, people today hunger for a deep spiritual experience. They seek to have everyday needs met. They want God to be part of their daily lives. They long to be part of communities not so much of doctrinal absolutism or social ascendancy but of authenticity. If they find this authenticity in a local church, they will come, and, in fact, they will come in great numbers.

The Pastoral Summit addressed those longings squarely in a series of workshops and discussions that demonstrated what is happening in some of the best churches in America.

The presenters at the Pastoral Summit were chosen from among the churches that were featured in two ground-breaking books: *Excellent Protestant Congregations: The Guide to Best Places and Practices* and *Excellent Catholic Parishes: The Guide to Best Places and Practices.* These books feature the three hundred Catholic and three hundred Protestant churches that were found in a nationwide search for church excellence.

These essays, adapted from the actual Pastoral Summit presentations, provide, if not a model, at least guideposts for any church seeking to answer common and sometimes vexing questions facing all churches. To name just a few, How to make enthusiastic disciples out of ordinary members; how to reach youth, Generation X, the unchurched, the untouched; how to impact the community in a significant way; how to create a truly welcoming environment; how to sense the needs of a congregation and effectively meet them.

These essays provide both information, but as importantly, inspiration for all churches. What comes through over and over again is that it is possible for every church to achieve excellence. For these presenters are not superhumans; their churches are as small as sixty and as large as ten thousand, their resources are not unlimited. These are churches just like yours, with similar problems and limitations.

What sets them apart is that they found new (and sometimes quite old) ways to connect with people and to spread the life-giving Word of God into a world that may seem oblivious, yet down deep yearns to live a life of goodness, faith, and, yes, authenticity. These people have placed their faith in the working of the Holy Spirit, and the results have been creative, innovative approaches to ministry that have profoundly changed lives.

Most of the presentations at the Pastoral Summit featured both a Protestant and a Catholic perspective, providing rich insights from each tradition. The premise of the Pastoral Summit was that the similarities among Catholic and Protestant churches far outnumber and outweigh the differences. This was confirmed over and over both in the presentations and in those conversations in the hallways. Protestant and Catholic paths to God may be different, but their goals are surely the same: to sanctify people and our world, to provide food, support, and companionship for the journey of life.

Included at the end of the book is a short biographical sketch of the presenters and their church so that you can put the information in a context. Contact information is provided should you want to continue, after you put the book down, your own conversation.

The simple premises behind the Pastoral Summit are that local churches are still where most people turn to for spiritual sustenance and support and that the strategies certain local churches use in transforming both individual lives and entire communities can be duplicated elsewhere. The Pastoral Summit sought to find and then hold up examples of church excellence so that they might be the seeds for new life and innovation in other churches.

That is the hope for this book; that local churches would see that they are already fertile soil and that, with faith in their members and in God, their possibilities are limitless.

Background on the Parish/ Congregation Study and the Pastoral Summit

In 1996, Paul Wilkes led a three-day mission at the Church of the Presentation in Upper Saddle River, New Jersey. Although he regularly writes about religion and religious belief, it was an experience unlike anything he'd ever had before. The church was exciting. The people loved to be there. They welcomed strangers into their community. The outreach and the reverence were *real*. The church had, in Flannery O'Connor's words, a "habit of being."

He wondered, were there not other churches like this one? And shouldn't people know about these authentic and deeply spiritual places? So began the Parish/Congregation Study, a two-year project funded by the Lilly Endowment based at the University of North Carolina at Wilmington, where Wilkes teaches, that searched the nation for excellent local churches. Wilkes and project associates Marty Minchin and

Melanie Bruce eventually found some six hundred excellent Catholic parishes and Protestant churches. They visited a representative number of them, spending time with the church's pastor, staff, congregation, and community, getting to know the people and experiencing the life of the church.

The Parish/Congregation Study staff was amazed at the variety of excellence found at the churches—from an innovative approach to rural ministry in Lone Wolf, Oklahoma, to a tithing parish in Wichita, Kansas, where every child receives a fully paid Catholic education to a church in Birmingham, Alabama, that is drawing the unchurched by the hundreds, to a parish in inner-city New Orleans that has brought hope and vision to its neighborhood and become a powerful force in the city.

Those churches and parishes are featured in two books: *Excellent Catholic Parishes: The Guide to Best Places and Practices* (Paulist Press) and *Excellent Protestant Congregations: The Guide to Best Places and Practices* (Westminster/John Knox Press). The books also contain a list of all the excellent churches in the study, successful—and reproducible—programs and approaches, and the common traits the study team found.

But the news about these life-changing, community-building churches demanded an even wider audience than the books. In conjunction with the Institute for Church Life at the University of Notre Dame, the Parish/Congregation Study research team created the Pastoral Summit, funded by a new grant from the Lilly

Endowment, so this wealth of information could be exchanged.

The Pastoral Summit, the first-ever gathering of Protestants and Catholics focused exclusively on the local church, was held May 30–June 1, 2001, in New Orleans. Clergy and lay people from the churches and parishes in the books were the workshop leaders.

Some seven hundred pastors, church staff, and lay leaders, from Catholic, mainline, and evangelical churches from Hawaii to Puerto Rico attended.

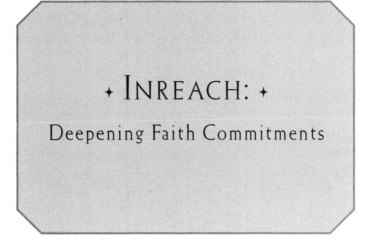

✦ INREACH: ✦

Deepening Faith Commitments

+

Reality-Based
Sermons:

A CATHOLIC PERSPECTIVE

+

FATHER PATRICK BRENNAN, pastor
Holy Family Parish, Inverness, IL

E vangelization, I have found, is what draws people to church. It might be done by word of mouth, the example of members, or advertising. The warmth of the congregation, the quality of the liturgy, music, and art are what keep them coming. And, very importantly, preaching. Wade Clark Roof, in his book *Spiritual Marketplace: Baby Boomers and the Remaking of American Religion*

(Princeton University Press), said that people come to a church seeking meaning, belonging, and a shared spirituality for their families. I would suggest folks also come to church because it offers healing and direction. Preaching that offers a livable spirituality can play a vital role in fulfilling these needs.

Effective preaching often leads with a story, which should center on some sort of human experience. This does not necessarily have to be a story about the preacher—it could be a story from the news—but either way, it is a story of human experience. This story is an attempt to connect with scripture, so that the arrow goes toward *the* story, the story of scripture. As the story unfolds, a counterstory is triggered and emerges in the congregation. The sermon begins to loosen experiences people in the congregation have had that are congruent with what the preacher is talking about. The congregation has a tangible experience of what I call the "intuition of the incarnation." They have an intuition of revelation that God is present in us, God is with us, breaking through and manifesting Himself to us. There is a felt urgency to respond.

I often hear evidence of these counterstories after the worship service, when parishioners make comments such as, "I felt you were talking to me today" or "How did you know couples go though that" or "That's a struggle in parenting." The counterstory moves to an intuition on the level of people's imaginations. We are breaking into the realm of God, and God is breaking into our realm.

Preachers should write homilies themselves and give themselves enough time to do it properly. I'm not the first to say this is the most important teaching you'll do all week. If anyone of us just sits down to crank out a homily, it is probably not going to be a good one, or worse. A homily has to emerge, and gradually it is pulled together and redacted. I have developed a discipline for this that begins with pre-viewing and remote preparation for a block of Sundays. At Holy Family Parish we produce a booklet called *Sharing Faith*, a copy of the scriptures for the coming Sundays that folks in our one hundred and thirty small Christian communities and ministering and leadership communities use. It is also has five or six faith-sharing questions for two to three months in advance. I am part of the Faith-Sharing Question team, which means I sit down with them several months in advance and look at the broad sweep of what is coming.

For a homily to emerge, I must look at the scriptures long before I begin to write. As for writing the homily itself, for the next Sunday I try to begin the emergence of the homily on the previous Monday. I write a bulletin reflection for every Sunday based on that Sunday's scriptures. This is the first articulation, writing of where I am going with the scriptures. Throughout the week at our staff meetings and all ministry meetings, we have a discipline in our parish called "Faith First." Before a group ever gets to the business of its meeting or gathering, members spend fifteen to twenty minutes looking at next Sunday's readings, doing one or two of the faith-sharing questions from the book, and offering petitions of prayer with each other. This means that several times during the week staff members, including myself, are with a different group talking about next Sunday's scriptures. We are getting that wisdom, that spirituality, that "lived faith" of folks as we read and talk through Faith First.

When I teach, either on the undergraduate or graduate level in the ministry schools I help out in, we also do Faith First. This may sound selfish, but I am constantly being fed by the faith of other people as they look at these scriptures throughout the week with me; people's convictions and experiences add to the mix of this emerging homily. This lectionary-based approach, which is also followed in our children's, high school, and adult ministries, provides built-in accountability for pastors. You are doomed if you are not prepared when you walk into that church when so many in the congregation have prayed over and broken open the same Word of God that you are preaching about. It is mandatory that homilies are well prepared in our parish.

I do not mean this narcissistically, but I believe that a homilist should never get too far from himself or herself when writing a sermon. Do not reach too far. Seminally, examine how the Word of God challenges and comforts you this week. I know the challenge and comfort that scripture brings to me, a pretty ordinary person, is probably the kind of challenge and comfort it might be bringing to other people.

Yet because I am a celibate priest, I *am* different. How can I relate to how God's Word challenges and comforts these people and what they are experiencing? Their marriages? Their parenting? Their lives as single people? Their lives as young adults? Their issues at work? Giving witness to how God's Word is comforting and challenging me can connect with these issues in the congregation. I am a man dealing with some of the same things they are dealing with. I encourage preachers to share some of their own struggles or stories of repentance and conversion. I frequently speak of the frustrations I have as the chief caregiver for my mother, who is 93. I refer to struggles I have had and still have with anxiety and depression. I just lost an aunt who I was very close to, which has really put me into a mode of grieving and missing her. I often mention that the older I get, the angrier I get, and I do not like that about myself. Life is a journey of repentance. I want folks to see that I do not live in a plastic bubble.

But in attempting to engage the emotions and experiences of your congregation in homily preparation, do not forget to also practice exegesis. This science is the movement backward that is crucial in preaching. What were the religious experiences of these people from whom these scriptures came? What was going on with them? We cannot just tell stories and leave out explanation and interpretation of the scriptures behind them. We must also engage in the art form of hermeneutics. How is the scripture to be interpreted today? Or how does this scripture help us to interpret today? Faith, in fact, is a way of interpreting experience. Discover a powerful ending for your presentation, for your homily both beginnings and endings if done well, are remembered.

We must also take into account our audience when preparing homilies. We are preaching to a psychologized generation that places a high value on feelings and emotions. When we examine scripture, we must ask: "What are the feelings that are encased in the passages that we are preaching about? What are the relational dynamics that might speak to us now? What did Jesus feel here? What was Peter feeling? What was Mary feeling? What was the woman in John 8 feeling? What were those guys with the stones in their hands feeling? How did Jesus challenge them?" We must weave the answers to these kinds of questions into our homilies.

To put a different spin on that approach, we can also learn from the school of psychology called *neurolinguistics* that teaches that all people communicate in three levels, or channels: the visual, the audio, and the kinesthetic. Most folks' method of communication involves a dominant channel and a secondary channel. The research shows that most of us block out the third channel, which we also need to develop. Visual people need to see things as they listen, and they want you to see things as they speak. Often the visual person will communicate in story form. Others communicate primarily with the audio channel. They like to hear things, and they think everybody else likes to hear things too. Often these are idea people. The third group communicates dominantly on the kinesthetic, or emotional, channel. These people operate on feelings.

It is not difficult to pick up what communication channel people are on. Visual people look up to see things. Audio people's eyes bounce between their ears. And kinesthetic people look like they have inferiority complexes. They look down a lot and pull up their feelings from a well inside. So if we are not sensitive to these three channels when we prepare and deliver homilies, we are losing bunches of people. I really believe that Jesus was visual, audio, and kinesthetic—he told stories that provoked powerful feelings and emotions and that also contained powerful, challenging ideas. It's selfish for us as preachers to just stay on our own channels. We must strive to minister to all of the channels that are before us.

As to the practical side of homily preparation, create a block of time, no later than Friday afternoon, for redaction. I spend between five and six hours in deliberate redaction. Writing homilies is an important discipline. Focus on the quality of the writing, creating a beginning that captures interest. In the body of the homily explore the human story, a breaking open of the scriptures, and its connection to the human story. This leads to personal application: "What should we do? How should we be?" Include examples of personal response as well as implications for parishioners' responses, compassion, and justice.

Leave a block of time for rehearsal. This might sound neurotic, but I would suggest rehearsing toward planned spontaneity, a homily that appears conversational and informal but is very well planned. My goal is to practice each homily to myself five times, moving toward soft memorization. In the rehearsal I try to discover power words that I am really going to milk. I create memory devices that will help me with the delivery. I do not preach from the pulpit. I preach from the stairs of the sanctuary. It is important to watch your timing, not just your length, but also the sense of the integrity of the homily. Does it flow? Does it hang together? Do not get lost on side roads that cause you to have a difficult time getting back on the main road.

Before giving the homily, pray. Throughout this holy emergence process, pray. I have to pray for God's help to feel good about myself. Do not let anxiety and nervousness get in the way. Let the motivation for the homily and its delivery be love, not, "I want to give a good homily." Ask God to help you to love this congregation and help you to give witness to the truth of the passages and the truth of God's presence among us. We are called to preach truth, and people need to hear truth. Cardinal Joseph Bernardin used to write a column in our local newspaper called "The Truth in Christ." These are important words when we preach. Preach the truth about Christ and about life.

When you deliver the sermon, communicate. Connect with your congregation emotionally, conversationally, and relationally; engage them, hold them, be strong, be humble, be wise, be humorous. Do not operate out of "I've got to get though this, I have to crank out another one"—that does not work. The Spirit prompts additions even as we speak, even as we are preaching. If it seems like a movement of the Spirit, grab it. Be open to the congregation and include them. This can also happen in the rehearsal stage. Evaluate yourself. What can you learn about theologizing and communicating? Seek out the evaluative comments of others. If a homily does not work well and you know that, seek out why. An effective homily does not necessarily mean people liked it or liked you message. A good homily could leave people very angry or uncomfortable.

✦

Reality-Based Sermons:

A PROTESTANT PERSPECTIVE

✦

REVEREND BILL ELDER, pastor
MountainTop Community Church, Birmingham, AL

A s preachers, we have all been taught to pray and to study scripture. But for sermons to be truly effective, to truly resonate with a congregation in a way that prompts thinking and change, we also have to be students of the experience of the reality of our own people. We cannot afford to get further and further away from our people, to spend forty-five minutes on an exposition that has no practical application to their lives.

When people who attend our church talk about what their impressions have been of MountainTop and why they have decided to join our church, gratefully they often refer to hearing a sermon that seemed to address their lives personally and specifically. After the sermon, I've heard that people will say, "Did Bill Elder call my wife?" or "Was Bill Elder peeking in my window this week?" That's what I want—for the sermon to be relevant, to pierce their lives and give them something tangible to consider.

But, my first response is always, "It's a God thing." The nature of biblical truth is that we have a relevant God who can cause the occasion of a sermon to connect, which I believe is the real bottom line. Reality preaching, I think, is a "God thing" because God is the ultimate reality. Naturally, there must be a divine/human partnership in place. What follows is an attempt to spot the human role in this communication partnership. I believe that although preaching is a spiritual gift, it is also a skill that has to be developed. As I consider my years as a teacher-preacher and as I have sought to be a junior partner with God in composing and delivering reality-based messages, a couple of handfuls of principles have surfaced for me—a kind of "top ten" list.

I have never experienced surfing, but I had a roommate in college who was from Hawaii. From what he told me about surfing, I now think of preaching as a similar practice. In a sense, what we must do as preachers is catch God's wave and ride it to shore. Here are some surfing tips on how to bring your congregation with you on an exciting and empowering ride.

1. Ride the big wave for at least a week.

Reality preaching begins with your reality, with your life. So, from scripture, first get clear in your own mind as to what the main idea for your sermon will be. Then, live with the idea all week, keeping pen, paper, and manila folder close at hand. I have discovered that God is quiet, and listening is really our job. I am constantly amazed at how God presents real life illustrations of that biblical truth as we live it, taking truth from the pages of the Bible and allowing it to come to life in our lives. In fact, when life and scripture connect, it's not just an "aha" moment, it's a miracle moment. And with that comes huge gratitude to God for speaking and passion for sharing what you've heard with others. That's how the message goes from head to heart, something that is crucial for connecting with your hearers.

As preachers, we must remember that we are part of a process that is much bigger and far more important than simply putting together a nice little talk. We must speak the truth that has shaped us first. This is the only way that what we present can be a transforming experience for our people. When we really live the truth ourselves, God brings out the breadth and the depth of the truth that we're dealing with in real life, fresh ways.

Give yourself plenty of time to consider and prepare your sermon. If you wait until the weekend to get this process going, you end up using sermon illustration books, Internet illustrations, and events that happened to you years and years ago. The message becomes more of a third-party reporting than a first-hand testimony. A first-hand account has far more power and freedom to it.

2. Share your experience on the board.

I have found that what our people appreciate most is when I share my own struggles with the "main idea" or the "main response"—the main idea that the sermon evokes. We need to speak with vulnerability, honesty, humility, and humor, while always avoiding both the spotlight and the pedestal. In First Corinthians 4:16, the Apostle Paul says, "Therefore I urge you to imitate me." I don't think Paul is writing out of arrogance or pride. Rather, this is inspired insight about spiritual leadership, about authenticity, and about practical communication. He is not saying, "Look at me, I have everything in perfect shape, all battles won."

If you are familiar with the character of Paul, you know that's not true. Quite the contrary, he calls himself the chief of sinners, the least of the apostles, and he admits to struggling with obedience. Paul is actually inviting the Corinthian Christians to join him on his discovery journey. He is saying, I am also growing and learning. You can look at my life—I do not mind. I am far from perfect, and I am not pretending or posturing that I am something else. My desire to follow Christ is real. I have learned that for spiritual leadership to work, my own walk with God will always be Exhibit A. As preachers, we want to avoid the pedestal but not the microscope. Our lives are our primary illustration. You cannot lead where you yourself are not going, and preaching is a vital part of that leading. We too must be able to say, "Be imitators of me as I seek to follow Christ."

What people respect and appreciate most is not perfection, but realness and sincerity and authenticity. Share your life, your journey, and your struggles, and be honest and vulnerable without being self-serving. Do not be two dimensional or contrived. Take no liberties with either your purity or the truth. Tell it like it is; do not shape it. Your personal righteousness—or at least your attempt at personal righteousness—is the most precious offering that you bring to God and to those you lead and teach and serve.

3. Preach the big waves, not the puny ones.

Time is precious, time is short, and life is fragile. People do not always return to church for more. I am not suggesting you can get everything said in one sermon, but I am saying that we must communicate high impact truth. For that to happen in my sermons, I have to be extremely clear about why the stakes are so high, why it is so crucial to "get this right." "No big deal!" preaching is best left unsaid.

When you prepare your sermon, look for the "knees" truth of the biblical text. That's the truth that catches fire in your heart and makes you feel like you have to get on your knees because you know you didn't come up with that insight on your own. God has been there with you, speaking. When you discover this kind of truth you know what revelation means. There is an insight there that you haven't seen before, and it changes and expands your understanding of reality. You have really heard God's voice. And you can hardly wait to share the message with your people. You just know that if they can get it, it will change their lives.

These experiences really do happen if you are open to them. You choose waves that you know can change people's lives, that can help them move from caterpillar to butterfly. If you are not exited about what you share, your hearers are not going to be either. And, if we are not exited, it is because we have not been to the mountain of God. And to return to the surfing metaphor, the truth is that God's waves are all big waves.

4. View the films and live the legacy.

When you present biblical characters in your sermons, give them three-dimensional lives. Let them come alive. Let your congregation see that these folks in the Bible had to handle life just we do. Their full humanity is there. You can find it if you take the time to wrestle with the text. And go ahead and flesh it out. There is nothing wrong with saying something like, "I know we do not have a complete novel-like description here, but here is my take on it."

For instance, in the story of Zacchaeus in Luke 19, the text does not describe what happens between the time Jesus accepted Zacchaeus as he was and the time Zacchaeus declares that he is giving half of what he owns to the poor. Something significant happened in that gap in the text, and I think it's perfectly okay to speak of what might have happened based on how we see Jesus operating and what we know about tax collectors. We need to flesh out the story for the congregation so they can recognize what Jesus was doing and how it transformed someone's life.

5. Coach throughout the ride.

Preachers of a former generation would spend forty-five minutes in precept instruction and exposition and then end with fifteen minutes of application. Those days have gone for good. Thanks to TV, *USA Today*, and the Internet, attention spans are now measured in nanoseconds. If you cannot make a point quickly, it is not going to get made. Therefore, application has to happen from the beginning and throughout the message because application is what keeps hearers engaged and attentive. If they can't see themselves in your message, they will quickly zone out. This kind of application must be real, not gimmicky or manipulative, such as throwing in a joke in to wake people up or constantly getting your audience to say little phrases to each other such as, "How many of you remember this? Raise your hand!" That's a far cry from life interaction.

I did a series once called "Taming our Tigers." The series idea was that there are things in life that we all have to deal with, that will never go away, and that have the potential to cause real damage. They need to be tamed rather than eliminated. Anger is one of those tigers. I talked about when Jesus and Moses got angry, appropriately angry. Then, instead of moving right on to another point, I said, "Listen up parents, there are a lot of kids who are real angry these days because their parents do not get angry about the right things." This was not the major point of my message, but I was tying it into their lives at the beginning of the sermon, trying to coach as I went along. My rule of thumb as I am writing my message is not to go more than two minutes without making some application.

6. *Know what you hope to experience.*

Preaching needs to be done with a clear purpose. We need to know what we hope our hearers will know when we finish and what we want them to do with the knowledge. We need to have it clear in our heads—"This is what God wants us to know, and this is what God wants us to do in response to this information." We can be sure of this—God wants to expand our understanding (enlighten) and transform our behavior (empower).

Once we know what we hope to experience we're ready to write. This directional, purposeful statement also helps others who are involved in planning services. In our church we have a six-member team of people that comes together each week to program the Sunday service. We plan about three weeks out. I spend about three hours each week with this team. Our job is to communicate the message using whatever support we can bring on line. We constantly marvel at the way God weaves everything together and expands the light and turns up the power. And this process relies tremendously on that initial functional vision of what God wants that experience to be.

7. *Get all the equipment you need for the ride.*

People learn globally today more so than any other time in history. If we rely only on the spoken word to communicate the message, we are surfing with outdated, under-strength equipment. At MountainTop, everything that happens on Sunday morning is a part of the surfing equipment. We use drama, movie clips, video, testimonials, interviews, staging, lighting, music, and sometimes even questions and answers after the message. For the "Taming Your Tiger" series, we had a stage set that looked like a jungle scene straight from *Jumanji*. Ushers wore pith helmets, and we placed tiger paws on the floor, pulling the theme together.

This week we dealt with the anger of laziness. When congregants arrived on one Sunday, the ushers were sitting down instead of standing up handing out bulletins. People were given blank pieces of paper rather than the usual program/bulletin. Then various staff members came to the stage and apologized for not being ready for Sunday's service. One said: "Look I am sorry about the bulletin, but I just didn't have time this week. Maybe I'll have time next week. We'll see." I stood up and told them that I had been out of town speaking and I didn't have time to prepare a sermon, and I told them I'd try to work in some sermon preparation time next week. Then the music cranked up, the ushers were on their feet and the real programs were distributed. And we were ready to talk about taming the tiger of laziness. It was all done in an effort to bring the message home in fresh, creative ways.

8. Get comfortable and balanced on the board.

When we present and deliver sermons, we must be comfortable with ourselves. Acting is not reality-based. It is one thing to act out a biblical person for a few minutes during a sermon, which I think can be very helpful, and then return to your real self. But if you are acting all the way though the message you are making a big mistake. People can easily see whether you are acting or presenting something that has really transformed you. Do not perform your entire message like a passage from Hamlet. People can spot actors immediately, and the result is that they appreciate the talent of good acting, but their lives are not changed by acting, no matter how polished and professional.

We are in the business of letting God use us to change lives, so just be real. We want to get real people in touch with the real God. Talk real. Help them become amazed at God, not at you. Avoid theological shorthand. Recognize that no matter how seasoned your believers are, they really do appreciate it if you will explain to them what you are talking about in conversational English. Of course, speaking for a seeker-targeted church, I try very hard to use only language that unchurched people will understand.

9. Do not play it safe.

Go for the big waves. That's the kind of God we have. Life with God is never boring. So, be bold, be candid. Speak the truth with love. But don't reshape the truth so that everyone will like it. Then it probably won't be the truth that you serve up.

Don't take the edge off of God's truth. I believe that is ministerial malpractice. Even worse, I believe we will one day answer to God for that. You can raise big issues. You can take your stand on them and then always allow people to find their own place to stand. You can say: "Here's where I come down on this. You can be a Christian and not come down exactly where I do, but I want to encourage you to really deal with this." Come down somewhere that makes sense biblically. People appreciate that honesty, that challenge, and that freedom.

10. Enjoy the ride.

This is absolutely my favorite part of being a preacher. Realize that God is the wave; he's the power that inspires and energizes you. And if you let him, he will carry you. If you think it is your talent that makes a difference, then you are on your own. Good luck in making your own wave. It's God's wave that carries us all the way from initial vision, through insightful preparation, through anointed presentation. Know this and know it is your job to work hard and partner with him. Go though the message many times before standing to speak, but then as you stand, relax and trust, balance out, and enjoy what He does with you and through you. It's an awesome experience. Of course it is. God is awesome.

When this is your process, you'll see God doing so much more than you could ever do or ever imagine. You just breathe a prayer of gratitude. "Thanks God, for letting me in on this." That's how it happens that you preach with passion, and joy, and others want to join you in the water and on the wave. What a ride!

+

The Stewardship
Way of Life

+

Father Thomas McGread, retired pastor
St. Francis of Assisi, Wichita, KS

It was my privilege to be in one parish for thirty-one years. During that time, the parish—St. Francis of Assisi—became somewhat famous because of the generosity of its parishioners. In those thirty-one years, I think I spoke about money five times. What I constantly talked about—five hundred or five thousand times—was community. We stressed the importance of people giving their time to Almighty God. We did surveys to find out what the needs of that community were. We asked people to volunteer for the care of those needs. We listened, and we honored their talents, their abilities, and their ideas. These parishioners became active people, and one of the things you realize is that once you get people involved in a parish they get a sense of belonging. Then they get a sense of ownership, and once they get a sense of ownership, they get a sense of responsibility. That is where the final part of the time-talent-treasure equation comes in. And only here, after time and talent have already been offered up to God, does the treasure come into play.

When I left that parish of two thousand families, the average collection was $84,500 per week. We had enough for a free Catholic education for every one of our kids, enough to fund our social outreach, and enough to take care of the normal needs of a parish. Here's how it began.

It was in 1972 that I changed the concept of stewardship from being a "program" or an "appeal" to stewardship being a "way of life." In our church we are inviting people to live their lives as God intended them to live according to the teachings of Christ that we find in the sacred scripture and to build up a personal relationship with Almighty God. It is logical, straightforward, and holy—and presented properly, it is easy for people to grasp and want to live.

Years ago, I had heard of two young priests in Mobile, Alabama—Father David Sullivan and Father

Joe Jennings—who were trying to come up with a Catholic theology for the Protestant idea of tithing. One of the things I noticed in their writing was the statement that "people are looking for standards in their lives," such as the type of home they live in, the type of education for their children, and the number of children they want to have. If we are looking for standards for life, then we must also be looking for standards in our relationship with God. This made a great deal of sense to me. But I knew that once you mentioned tithing at all in church, you lost about half of the audience.

When I initially approached the subject, I talked about tithing as an ideal from Almighty God because it is mentioned so many times in the scriptures. I didn't begin with the tithing of money, but the tithing of time. I began with asking the people in the church how much quality time husbands and wives should give to each other. How much time should they—or did they—give to their children in their homes. Sometimes children in the best Catholic homes can be neglected because of their parents' busy lives. I once read a survey that showed that the average father spends all of seventeen minutes with each child during a week. Now, while people have different amounts of money, everyone has time. We are all busy, but we have time for TV, newspapers, magazines, playing sports, and talking on the phone. I asked people to reflect on where they were "spending" their time.

Then I asked, "How much time do you give God at home?" The home is a little church where we find a personal relationship with Almighty God. Once you get it into people's minds to give some time to God at home, then you will find that the activities of the church will become very important and more natural to them, because it is in church where we find Christ in the Mass and in the Eucharist.

As the scriptures tell us, on judgment day we will be asked to account for ourselves, what we have coveted, and what we have shared. "When I was hungry you gave me to eat. When I was thirsty you gave me to drink. When I was naked you clothed me. When I was ill or imprisoned, you came to visit me." This refers not only to the needy on the streets, but the needy within our homes, among the parish community, and in our cities. For Jesus said, "As long as you did it for the least of my little ones, you did it for me."

I made it clear that each and every one of us will stand there alone. We will be asked the same questions: What did we really do for one another? It will never be asked how much faith we had, or how much power we had or how much influence we had in the world. But we will be asked what we did for one another. This is of course one of the reasons we have churches in the first place, to provide a way so we truly can help one another in our lives.

So, when people began to see time as valuable and that they needed to allot some of it for both their family and their church, that they would be listened to and their input and talents would be appreciated, it was then time to talk about tithing part of the wealth that God had apportioned to them.

I didn't think it was good to simply talk about tithing without having some specific needs, and as Catholic education has always been important to me, I talked about education just as we were establishing our grade school. Many people realized that they would not be able to send their children to the school if they were charged tuition, which goes up year after year. And, the people who had school-age children at that particular time were the least likely to have money to afford to educate them. It's the people who already have their children educated or the ones who have not even started yet that can afford to do that. That is why we made education a mission of the parish and a mission of a community. In doing so, everyone in the parish was totally involved.

We now have more than eight hundred students, and we have all lay teachers in that grade school. In addition, every parish child is also guaranteed four years of Catholic high school education—all paid for by the parish. We have very wealthy people as well as single-parent families on welfare, but when the stewardship way of life sets in, there is always enough for everyone.

The one thing that we tell them with regard to their money is that they are not giving it to the church for any purpose. They are giving it to God. They are returning it to God in thanksgiving for what He has done for them. It is very important that we talk about it in that particular way. The practice of tithing is mentioned thirty-nine times in the Old Testament, eleven times in the New Testament. It is a guide for people to work up to. And I do encourage people to use percentage giving. We do not use amounts, because some people may be frightened when they realize their $10 a week may show up as .5 percent of what they should be doing. Percentage giving truly encourages people to get on par with Almighty God. All the gifts we have come from God. It is hard for us to realize this at times.

I have taught stewardship in three different parishes: one of 50 families, the second of 350 families, and the third started with 650 and was at 2,000 when I left. So the size of the parish is not an issue. In each place, one thing that was particularly interesting to me was the fact that the stewardship way of life really helped church attendance. We estimated from head counts that 85 percent were there every Sunday. The national average is 41 percent. Again, there is that sense of ownership. People wanted to be in church because it was *their* church.

After the community of St. Francis of Assisi had shown that the stewardship way of life was possible, in 1985 our bishop asked us to extend this way of life to the entire diocese. At that time, the average weekend attendance across the diocese was between 60 and 65 percent. Last year, it was 78 percent. We got people to come back to church because each and every person gets an invitation each year to become a steward in God's kingdom. And now, every child in the diocese who wants to attend a Catholic school can attend kindergarten through high school free. The parish assessments going to the diocese were more than $15 million in 1985. The income now is more than $45 million a year, a tremendous increase. And we do not have special collections; we do not have a Bishop's Appeal. We have no special fund-raising programs. We take the money from the source, freely and thankfully given, and there is always enough to meet the needs.

When introducing the stewardship way of life, one of the first things to do is to choose the right people for the stewardship committee. This should be made up of positive people in the parish. You do not need any negative, foot-dragging, nay-saying committee members on a stewardship committee. But also, you do not need any finance people on the stewardship committee. This is because it may be misconstrued that all you are trying to do is to get people's money. All the members I chose were couples who attended daily mass. You can find these people right at the church door; there is no need to do a lot of research. You visit with them and discover that they are positive and that they love the church and will do anything for the church. I spent six months with my first group introducing this concept of stewardship before we put it into effect in the parish, teaching them strictly from the Bible. If you read the Bible, nineteen of Christ's major parables relate directly to stewardship. A steward is a manager, someone who looks after someone else's property. That is what we are, really. We are all managers in God's kingdom, and we have a responsibility to protect and to expand God's gifts.

Once people acquire this sense of responsibility, it becomes a part of their way of life and goes into everything they do. For example, if everyone practiced stewardship, we wouldn't need environmentalists. We could protect the environment if we looked at it as a gift from God. That is what a stewardship way of life will teach us along the line. It is a way of life, and if we adopt it, we find that God is never outdone in generosity. God will always find for us the time to do what we really want to do, and he will provide the means we need. I have realized after all these years that if parishioners adopt the stewardship way of life for a year, they will continue throughout the remainder of their lives.

Once people have caught the spirit, it's very important that they be allowed to express what they think are the needs of the parish and the community. This is a dynamic situation, constantly changing; parishes have different needs. I find out those needs by surveys, but ask for no names. If you let people do this anonymously, you will get a more honest response.

For instance, one of the doctors in the parish came to me and was worried about the children who had no insurance. The doctor was concerned about something as simple as the children not receiving their inoculations. So we founded the Guadalupe Clinic, named after a closed parish school that was given to us to use for the clinic. Some 2,500 people go through the clinic each six months. We have more than forty doctors, more than seventy nurses, and dieticians. We have contacts with dentists, specialists, and the three hospitals in the city. Last year, more than one hundred surgeries were performed with no cost to the patient. We have interpreters, mostly Spanish and Vietnamese. And we have expanded the clinic to another part of town.

We know there are many people in this community who will need this kind of medical care, and we have been able to support it entirely by private donations. The people are generous, and the spirit of the stewardship way of life is contagious. Our diocese is building a diner that will feed the poor of Wichita every night; it is estimated around 350 will come, and this will be entirely operated by volunteers. All the contractors and architects are volunteers. The city commissioners came by and offered to serve one night a month.

People want to give, and they are willing to listen to the Gospel mandates, if these mandates are presented properly. Time, talent, treasure: You hear those words all the time. But if you begin with the stewardship of time, then talent and treasure will naturally follow.

Retreat—and Then Advance

REVEREND MARK BECKWITH, rector
All Saints Episcopal Church, Worcester, MA

In April 1999, I finally acknowledged to myself that I was worn out. More than anything else, it was the unrelenting pastoral load that tired me out. I felt weighed down. I was angry with the distress of others. I was angry with myself for being angry with them. My fatigue was such that I couldn't shake their distress from my own. I wondered if I could continue in parish ministry. I knew my upcoming and much-needed sabbatical leave would give me a chance to look at the world in a new way—not so that I could be refreshed as a pastor, but because I entertained the hope that I could develop enough clarity and energy to begin a different career.

But after my three-month absence, I didn't abandon the ministry. I did learn the real meaning of the spiritual discipline of *displacement,* an idea first introduced to me by the great Christian thinker Henri Nouwen at a class at Yale Divinity School in the mid-seventies. Displacement involves taking yourself somewhere else, either close or far away, for the purpose of being in relationship with God in a new and different way. Because you are in a different space emotionally, physically, or psychically, God appears in a different way. For ministers, displacement can be the anecdote to burnout.

Displacement can be practiced in a number of ways. Years ago, while in seminary, I went through a difficult time, to the extent that I was unable to pray. Henri Nouwen said to me: "Why don't you just lie down and not work so hard? If you start to cry, let that be your prayer, if you fall asleep, let that be your prayer." He gave me the permission I needed to step away from my distress, which was a step of displacement. That was a long time ago, and in my twenty-two years of ordination and work as a pastor, I have continued to learn how the practice of displacement can renew, refresh, and reconnect me with God.

I spent a year thinking about how I would spend my 1999 three-month sabbatical, which is a somewhat common practice in the Episcopal Church. I knew that I wanted to go away but not for an extended time, because I had a wife and two children at home who were happy to have me go for a while, but not for too long. The credit in the family bank goes down the longer you stay away, and I didn't want it to go below zero. I needed to spend some time alone, and I needed to spend some time in community with family, with other pilgrims and with God.

The first portion of my sabbatical quickly cleared up my original intention to figure out another career pursuit. At an eight-day Episcopal conference called CREDO, an acronym for Clergy Reflection Education Discernment Opportunity, I evaluated my personal, financial, physical, emotional, and spiritual life though a series of exercises with thirty other people. This helped me clarify what I am about and what is important. Indeed, I found out that my evangelical interest and what I had been doing for the last twenty years was what I ought to be doing, which was a nice thing to discover. It was completely fortuitous that this program began the sabbatical—and it helped me to frame the rest of my time.

I then did an eight-day silent retreat in a Jesuit retreat house in Wernersville, Pennsylvania, an experience that was extremely formative for me. I spent a half hour every day with a gifted spiritual director, who gave me a series of scripture readings to meditate on and offered feedback on those meditations. By the third day in silence, the demons began emerging and were dancing all over my psyche such that I couldn't sleep. Demons that I had not heard from in fifteen to twenty years were making a lot of noise and very troublesome. They were demons of shame and vilification—drawing out painful memories that I long thought had been dealt with.

In the course of that retreat, not being Roman Catholic but being in a Roman Catholic environment, I met the Virgin Mary everywhere I went, in the liturgy and pictures, everywhere. After five or six days I thought: "Who is this person? She has never been a part of my pious life or my prayer life." In the course of those eight days, I developed a relationship with Mary for the first time, and I discovered that here is a person, perhaps more than any other, who was available to God, and her availability to God became a model for me and my relationship with God. I also discovered that it is not my weaknesses that bring me away from God as it is as much my strengths, the parts that I feel most confident about and that I feel I do the best. In my strengths I can easily fall into hubris and a subliminal feeling that I don't need God at all. In the course of eight days with the spiritual director, I developed my own mission statement, which has been very important to me and my ongoing prayer life. As I moved deeper into mystery, the demons disappeared.

After a couple of weeks at home, I spent a week at Taize in France, an ecumenical community that gathers pilgrims from all over the world. While at Taize, I worshipped with about one thousand people three times a day, singing chants that were repeated dozens of times with no sense that they had a clear end. In the middle of each daily service, this international group of one thousand spent ten minutes in silence. On the second day, that silence became absolutely disarming to me. I discovered that silence is the universal language, and it spoke in a depth and profundity that I had never experienced before. I had spent a lot of time in silence by myself, but I had never done silence often with other people. While at Taize, I was able to yield to that silence and feel the full depth of it and discover that language that we all have in common.

I then went to California with my family, touring up and down the coast, celebrating our life together and our relationships that continue to change as our children get older. I returned from my sabbatical with two insights and two changes in my life. I felt these two insights my first day back. The first insight is that God does all the work. I know this and I have known this, but I really understood it when I came back from three months away worrying about the state of my church and found everything was pretty much in order. The congregation did not need me as much as I thought they did, which actually was a wonderful gift. I realized that God does the work, and sometimes I help. Many times I pursue ministry willfully rather than willingly.

The second insight was that I discovered that I do not have to prove myself to myself, to the congregation, or to God. I have spent most of my life needing to prove myself. God is not interested in my performance. When I was able to step back from that need to prove myself, I was able to let God manifest himself in the life of the congregation. I could stand back and let things happen without needing to micromanage them, without needing to be in charge of them, a transition that was incredibly liberating for me.

There are changes that have emerged since I returned from my sabbatical. I like to think that I work less. My wife say that I do not, and I think she keeps better track of this than I do. But I know I do not work as hard emotionally—I do not carry the work in the same way. Those distressed people in the congregation are still as distressed as they were two years ago, but their level of distress does not live in or on me the way that it did. I now recognize this need for retreat, this need for pilgrimage, and this need for displacement on an ongoing basis.

I get a three-month sabbatical every six years, and I can't wait until the next one. Until then, I have found other ways to practice displacement. I am a fellow of St. John the Evangelist, an Episcopal monastery in Cambridge, Massachusetts, that has its historical roots in England. I go there, overnight, once a month. I used to go just to see my spiritual director for an hour, cramming three hours for the drive and the meeting into an already very full day. These days, I leave mid-afternoon the day before I see my director and spend time at the monastery afterward. That displacement has been a gift to me, and my close friends in the congregation tell me what a gift it is to them as well because I am not the driven person that I would be otherwise if I do not take retreat.

As I returned to congregational life, I became more and more intrigued with the idea of establishing a rule of life in the congregation. As in any congregation, members' relationship with the church and with God differs widely. Some people are at church all the time and want to be there. There are folks who show up on Christmas and Easter and wander in at other times. There is a core of people who want to go deeper in their relationship with God, and what we offer week in and week out is good, but not enough. In thinking about developing a rule of life for people who are interested in the congregation, I have heard some models of this, but I do not know of many. I worry that if we have people who say they are members of a congregational order, they will be regarded as an elite crowd in the congregation and thus they will see themselves over against others, or others will see them as being different. This is something I have to think about and work through.

As the chaos of life increases, we are finding the spiritual hunger on the part of people is enormous. The Eucharist is foundational and is incredibly important, but there needs to be that and more. The Bible is important and needs to be engaged at every possible level, but there needs to be more living in community and struggling with community. People want to be more connected and to displace more because the traffic of life is increasing, the chaos of life is increasing. Life is getting more difficult to live in the relationship with God to which we are called, and we need these opportunities to engage in this God who gives us such abundant life.

EVANGELIZING:

Effectively Connecting with Your Community

Rural Churches
as Missionary
Outposts

REVEREND BILL GEIS, pastor
Lutheran Ministries of Southwest Oklahoma,
Lone Wolf, OK

In my travels across America visiting rural churches, I find many in survival mode, in a state of desperation, which is essentially just a slow path to death. Why can't rural churches, instead of settling for being fatalistic survivors, see themselves as the true missionary outposts they are? And in doing so, come out on top for the Lord's sake and for the sake of millions of people who are lost without Christ. There is a spiritual hunger in the land, and it is here in rural America as well as in large cities. It is a hunger that knows no geography, and we in rural ministry need to rethink how we look at the work we do, for it has changed, and changed radically.

In my experience, I have found that approaching rural ministry as establishing missionary outposts, not unlike those set up in foreign lands worldwide, can yield amazing results. Rural people often feel like city folk don't understand them—and haven't indigenous people said this for centuries as we came to "save" them? My job, as a pastor in rural ministry, is to take nothing for granted, to almost forget what I've read in books or learned in seminary. Instead I must look deeply at the people I am called and privileged to serve, understand their culture as best I can, and shape my ministry likewise.

Pastors and churches in rural areas first must build genuine, trusting relationships with those *outside* the Christian community. There is a huge breech of trust between the traditional Christian church and the average Joe and Jane on the street, just like there is between newly arrived missionaries in other cultures. We have to forge relationships that build trust.

In Lone Wolf, our congregation had a ninety-year history yet was hardly known or understood in the community. We make a conscious effort to bring ourselves to the community rather than the community to us. We held events at the "Old City Hall," the Community

Center, and the public school. Often these places were more inconvenient for us and not always the best suited, but going off campus was critical. We had free meals at special events rather than fundraisers. We engaged other Christian churches cooperatively. There was no one secret for success. It took time, some "turning of the other cheek" with critical people, and a determination to be a church serving the community whether or not that brought numerical growth to our congregation.

We have to be genuine. We have to be ourselves. The average Christian does not have many friends outside of the Christian community. You have to be intentional about reaching into the community and showing people that you are both human and you are seeking something that just may be what they also are seeking—though they may not know how to say it. Good church programs and Sunday morning services are not enough. Yes, they're important. They will provide some of the "staying power" and effective discipling of Christ followers, but people outside of the Christian community rarely start there. Christians "seek" a great church. People outside of the Christian community—and those who have left it—"seek" genuine relationships, not church programs, meetings, and performances.

I believe that Christians need to do less inviting of people to church and more living testimony of how Jesus *is* changing their lives. I say "is," present tense, something ongoing, not merely a past conversion event. When a Christian invites someone to his or her church, the implied message is "see the pastor," "hear the music," or "experience the program." No matter how dynamic the setting is, it's still institutional rather than relational. People need to meet Jesus through relationships. They don't need their friends to say, "Come meet other Christians"; they need their friends to be transparent enough to show them the Christian standing in front of them. They've got to be honest enough to admit that they too are still in the struggle, that they have questions, doubts, and fears. Nix the pious platitudes; show them how a relationship with Jesus is changing your behavior and outlook on life. Then the Christian church will be a place that the outsider considers worth risking. It can be that supportive community, that place of renewal and inspiration, and that experience of sharing in the body of Christ—but only when their Christian friends first "get real."

Like successful missionaries have always done, you don't send in wave after wave of missionaries. Pastors and rural missionary churches must raise up leadership from the locals rather than import them. Many denominations have pastor and clergy shortages, especially in rural areas. And many people bemoan this. I think that God is saying something to us. The "natives" are more likely to trust one of their own than someone who has come from afar "to save them from their ignorance." Successful missionaries became a part of their community before anyone was saved. And they were humble enough to realize that they would probably save very few. It would be the leaders they raised up from within that community who God would use to affect radical transformation in the community.

Although there will always be a need for professional church workers, clergy, and otherwise, the church must add flexibility to its training and educational tracts. The focus must not remain solely on a professional clergy. We must invest in the natives, raising up leaders locally, training them locally (or through distance technologies), and turning them loose locally. People who live among their communities are bigger stakeholders. Whereas a foreign, imported clergy may affect the lives of a few, local people will affect the lives of many. Hear this clearly clergy and seminaries: your jobs are not at risk, you're needed more than ever, but we need you to mobilize the laity to a higher calling.

Carl George, a church growth expert and author of numerous books, said, "The church of the future will form clusters in which they will provide their own seminaries." I heard him say that in 1993. It scared me at first. I feared for my own rural setting. How would we ever accomplish this? Nearly a decade later, that's what we are doing, and it's our greatest hope. We're seeking partnership with educational efforts both formal and informal, from seminaries to para-church groups, from the lecture/seminar circuit to our community colleges. We're crafting an educational model to train people to lead ministry. It's messy, but it's working. Everyone on my staff today is of local roots and trained through these kinds of partnerships along with my personal mentoring.

Missionary pastors and churches must support the building or rebuilding of community infrastructure. In rural America, the infrastructure, things like streets and roads, is falling apart. The services to rural America such as heath care—especially mental health care—school systems, and even the infrastructure of relationships within rural comminutes have deteriorated over the last ten years. Rural values, like a strong sense of community, the feeling of safety from crime, and pride in one's work are starting to disintegrate as well, largely due to a lot of economic and emotional pressures going on in people's lives.

A primary job of foreign missionaries has always been to help develop a community, helping the local people build wells or plant crops. Rural missionary churches and pastors have to rebuild their towns, but in a supportive role, not an aggressive role. We immediately went to work on being contributors to the rebuilding of family and the lives of children. We became active, informal partners with our school, offering after-school ministries that included values and faith building as well as academics such as science and history lessons. We taught kids to work on cars and how to plant gardens. We taught them woodworking and ceramics. We engaged them and affirmed their lives by our love, our time, and our mentoring. Every chance we could, we'd try to involve their parents. We got involved in cleaning up the community. We part-

nered with counseling services and civic youth programs. We listened to the needs of governing bodies
and worked to support and rally support around
them. And oftentimes, we found the dollars to make
these things happen.

Whereas foreign missionaries have to translate
English into the local language, rural missionaries have
to translate God's message into one that is relevant to
that culture. If you are in a preaching or teaching role,
you have to understand the language of the people and
what interests them. You have to go to the movies,
watch TV, and know what is happening. Even though
sometimes it is offensive, you have to know. Listen to
what kids and youth are saying. Listen as a researcher,
not a critic. Go to the school of culture, not as judge,
but as the heart that's looking for "every opportunity
to share your hope" (1 Pet 3:15).

It costs money to do ministry, and America is the most
expensive mission field in the world. There are incredible issues of dollars here. Missionaries rarely raise
money from the natives—their funding comes from the
faithful. That means that the fundraiser in a town to send
your youth to Guatemala does not quite make sense. You
have to be creative when you raise funds and find sources
outside of your community. Often this comes in the
form of sponsorship—about $40,000 of our operating
budget comes from individuals and organizations that I
have courted to fund our ministry.

The vast majority of our funds are from denominational leaders who have gone out on a limb because they

believe in what we are doing. I give my time voluntarily to denominational efforts and the relationships formed in those activities bring great dividends to the ministry. Others are people who have followed our ministry, visited us, and caught the fever of what we are doing. They just want to be a part of this.

Frankly I need to be more assertive about this. While many have abused appeals for money in the church, missionary leaders must be the resourcers of ministry—including funding. We need to be unapologetic about asking people to support the work of extending Christ's kingdom, of sharing with our brothers and sisters in the trenches, of taking risks in those nonconventional approaches to ministry.

Missionary leaders have to court the local leaders. I am not sure why in America we start a ministry at the crisis level. I've witnessed many new missions— especially cross-culturally—with food pantries, aid, and crisis centers. Great! I believe in that, but making the connections with leaders is where I see the place to start. You begin with leadership. The love of Christ obviously demands that charity follow. In American society today, I see very little charity in raising up leaders. I see charity raising up followers and dependants. When you ask God for leaders that's when things start happening exponentially. This is not how we do it when we go into other countries. There, missionaries go to the chief, to the leaders who give permission, and then they undertake whatever needs to be done, the crises that are at hand. It is not that we do not want to care for people in crisis, but often times we are starting at the wrong level. We want to start with the people who have influence on the community and transform the entire community, leaders like the superintendent of schools, the mayor or city manager, law enforcement, the people (and their descendants) whose names are on the dedication plaques and memorials in the community—people who are the energy behind the community and its history.

Missionary pastors and churches often raise other missionaries assuming that no one else is coming. But in all our denominations we are so uptight about inter-Christian relationships. As soon as you go abroad, you soon see that local people don't care if you are Lutheran or Catholic or Baptist as long as what you are doing has merit, as long as you yourself stand for something they can believe in, as long as you are meeting their needs. We should not be competing with the church down the road; we should embrace its people. We ought to assume that no one else is going to help us, so we are going to need each other. The more we develop relationships with other churches in our rural communities, the more we share our ministries and resources, the better we can reach our community.

Missionaries picture the world tremendously different than the average person; that is why a lot of churches are taking people to other countries for mission experiences for a week or a few weeks. They do this to help open their eyes to a view of the world that is so much bigger than they ever considered. Suddenly arguing over the color of the carpet does not matter. Our work in rural churches is not just the tending of our own neat little back yard and making sure that all the committees report on time.

Instead we need a new vision of rural America as a mission field, often in desperate need. Then we can look at the bigger picture and begin infusing these communities with life and hope.

Simple Ways to
Spread the Faith

Sister Clara Stang, O.S.F.
Catholic Area Parishes, Benson, MN

"Evangelism" is a word that has a strange sound to Catholics, an uncomfortable sound. It is something many Catholics run away from, thinking that "evangelism" means passing out Bible tracts or preaching on a street corner.

This is true in much of Catholic America, and certainly true in rural Minnesota, where I have served much of my ministry. In rural areas, everyone is supposed to know everyone; you are supposed to know their religion, their religious beliefs, everything about them. And in rural areas, it oftentimes is considered bad form to ever tell someone about your own faith—or to inquire about theirs.

I have found that although rural people may know each other on the surface, they do not always know what is going on in the deepest part of a person. Actually, rural people are ready for someone to enter their life with a message that will help them to live more meaningfully or to face a certain difficulty. In a word, they are willing, and they are waiting, to be evangelized. So often people feel locked up in their small world that has no windows, no way for light to come into it. This is where "creative" evangelism comes into play. And although I use the word "creative," I should really use the word "simple," because that's exactly what this kind of evangelism is. To begin with, you don't need a lot of special training for it; you don't need to be a person of towering, unshakable faith. But you do need to be a person who believes in the basic goodness of people and who feels inside that you have something that can be good for another person.

Creative evangelism has more to do with the ordinary than we think. Creative evangelism is regular people, like us, helping each other to connect everyday life and faith regularly. The *ordinary* is very important—evangelism is not just from the top down or for certain people. Our God continues to reveal Himself to all of us by telling us, often through others, who we can become. God does this daily and in simple ways, without loud fanfare. The ordinary people through whom God chooses to speak are those who choose to listen in a way that is real, who listen because they care. The trust level grows as these people set aside their own agendas to receive and understand what others are saying. One of our parishioners did this so well when a person whose demeanor was rather harsh and pessimistic joined the parish. This parishioner made special efforts to include her, affirm her, and be with her. Soon, the harshness and pessimism mellowed. Oftentimes, the most significant steps in evangelism are those that seem the most simple and are sometimes overlooked. It is what we do to help one another and connect our faith with life. Oftentimes, the most significant steps in evangelism are those that seem the most simple and are sometimes overlooked.

We have found that some Catholics have been angry or frustrated at the Church; they are confused and have faith questions. In our Catholic Area Parishes, we annually (usually during Advent) reach out with a published invitation in the local newspapers, radio stations, and church bulletins for anyone who has been away from the Church or who is angry because of their "Catholic experience," or who may have drifted from the Church for whatever reason to come "home for Christmas." We tell our active parishioners that the majority of inactive Catholics are looking for an invitation to come back. They need to know that they are cared about, that they are missed. Such an invitation is great evangelism, whether they do or do not choose to return right then. We invite active parishioners to accompany them to this meeting. We also invite a few others who have recently returned to church to join them for this open forum session. As a facilitator for such a gathering, I try to create an atmosphere of welcome and hospitality. By establishing a spirit of trust and confidentiality, and by speaking from the heart, others soon feel free to open up. It's a time to listen, to be quick to apologize for Church failures and slow to judge; always remembering that those who are hurting tend to think more with their emotions than with their heads.

Through such experiences I've learned that the reasons for giving up on the Church fall into three categories: Church laws (divorce, inferior status of women in the Church, birth control); personal abuse or hurts (real or perceived misunderstanding or mistreatment with a pastoral leader); or change (not understanding or accepting certain changes, or a desire for more change, or a sense that the Church let them down).

It's a beautiful experience, as people gather to support one another and share their hurts. At the end of the session, we invite them all to come back to the Church. We make ourselves available for further one-to-one pastoral guidance. It's always amazing how the mood in just one evening shifts from fear and apprehension to relief, hope, and gratitude. A card I received after one of those evenings expressed it this way: "In my heart I knew it was time to come back but I was afraid and didn't know how. I found Jesus in your open door and open hearts. Thanks!" We always have some people who have returned through such an experience.

Outside of these formal meetings, active parishioners are asked to be willing to answer questions or complaints about the Church. I always tell people not to be shy about this. You know more about your faith than you might think you do. Try to answer that question or complaint with as much information as you have, and if you need a more complete answer, tell the person you're willing to find out.

Hospitality is another tool we use to enhance and practice evangelism. Ceremonies that mark passages of life, such as weddings and funerals, are excellent opportunities to evangelize. We still follow the old custom of the church serving funeral dinners to families of the deceased. These are unique times when people who are unchurched or have been away from the church have a special opportunity to experience church. We, the people of our parishes, offer support by bringing the meal, serving it, and often visiting and eating with the grieving family.

The young parents in our community provide an excellent point of evangelism, particularly at the time of baptism. This is an opportune time because as new parents, they are often at a point where they are ready to include God and the Church in their lives. When they come to us and ask for baptism for their child, we do the baptism at their home. This is a much less threatening environment, and it shifts the focus of seeing baptism preparation from something academic to seeing baptism as a life to be lived. We sit around the kitchen table and talk about what baptism means to them and why they want to have their child baptized. I've learned how quickly and easily one can get to know a couple in this safe environment. It provides an opportunity to challenge, support, and encourage them as young parents. In rural Minnesota, the pastoral needs of new parents vary and sometimes are multiple. The baptism preparation process gives us the opportunity to talk to them about becoming active church members and about Christian parenting in many concrete ways.

One of the strengths of this baptism program is that the responsibility is placed on the parents. First, we give the parents a teaching/learning guide; *God's Own Child* (Twenty-Third Publications) by Bill and Patty Coleman, which provides education and an opportunity for them to talk with each other about what it means to have their child baptized. When they have completed those materials, they contact us. We visit with them again to hear their understandings, to relate to their concerns, to affirm them in their new role as Christian parents, and to plan the baptism ceremony. They see that the Church has a human face, that it is interested in their personal stories and that they are not just being mass-produced on some sort of religious assembly line.

One essential element of evangelization is making sure that people feel like they belong. People need to feel welcome, both at church and into their community. We visit new people in our area with a welcome basket and/or informational handouts. We have a reception for new members so that they can be introduced to the community. We also have area befrienders, volunteers who are helpful friends to people who are most in need. Befrienders meet on a regular basis for support, prayer, and coordination. They visit the sick, the homebound, and the elderly; they activate prayer lines and organize support gatherings for the grieving. Once a year the befrienders and I send a personal invitation to a next of kin to everyone in our area parishes who has died that year asking them to invite their families to "An Evening to Remember." They are asked to bring some remembrance (a photo or something made by or for the deceased), which is then used as part of our gathering ritual. The evening includes prayer, storytelling, and a short presentation and discussion on coping with loss and dealing with grief. Lots of peer ministry happens as they share their stories, memories, losses, and coping skills.

One of the easiest yet most effective ways we have found to evangelize is to simply ask people to come to church, to a small-group meeting, or to a church dinner. You would be surprised how many people just need a personal invitation to prompt them to get involved—they are just waiting to be asked. One parishioner tells a story of a time he asked a couple to join a newly organized Small Christian Community. To his surprise, they accepted. At they group's first meeting, he asked them why they did. They replied, "Because you asked us."

As a pastoral team we make efforts to be active in the civic community. This includes activities such as social gatherings of students, county fairs, and ecumenical endeavors such as Habitat for Humanity. For example, I helped organize and lead an ecumenical "Swift County Anti-Racism Task Force" that continues to organize activities to increase understanding and dismantle racism in our area.

To be effective, evangelism requires continuous faith formation, a life-long shaping that happens both in our church activities and worship and privately, as people pray. Our relationship with God is not just God and I, but God and we, so we must share prayer and worship together. One way we practice this is with a lectionary-based weekly scripture prayer, which we created ourselves based on the format in Art Baranowski's book, *Faith Sharing in Small Church Communities* (St. Anthony Messenger Press). The format is straightforward: an opening prayer, the scripture references from the lectionary, a short simple commentary, followed by three or four focus questions for faith sharing, a time for shared prayer, and a closing prayer. The weekly focus questions are key. They are created by some of our own parishioners, who make sure the language is not churchy and truly connects our ordinary life with faith.

To illustrate: For a healing Gospel (Mark 5:21–31) the focus questions were: (1) When were you recently touched by someone's cares? (2) What daily routines drain you? (3) Where do you go to get re-energized? (4) What attracts you to Jesus in this Gospel? Each week the scripture references and focus questions for the upcoming week are published in the church bulletin and on our web site, www.catholicareaparishes.org, for all to use at home and/or at their gatherings. We use the scripture prayer guide at our own pastoral team meetings, parish and finance council meetings, and all parish committee meetings. This commonality connects our life, and our faith, weekly. All of this helps our people to come into worship on Sunday quite prepared. Invariably people will remark how great it is to come to Mass prepared. They come to celebrate the Word and to hear the homily, and they often find themselves continuing the sharing at home after Mass.

We follow a similar format with our annual Lent/Easter reflection booklet, which is mailed to the nine hundred households of our area's five parishes. As early as mid-October we elicit sixty volunteers (men, women, youth, student classes, and families) and give them a specific scripture reference from the Lent/Easter season. They are asked to pray about it and respond with a one hundred- to one hundred fifty-word reflection or prayer. Their reflections are typed into a "page-a-day" booklet. Volunteers collate and prepare the booklets for mailing. We have done this for the last eight years now, and the response continues to be positive and inspirational. In a rural parish where people know each other, they are proud and amazed at how God speaks through each reflection. The color of the booklet cover varies from year to year, and to my amazement some have saved the entire eight-year series. Truly, these booklets are filled with expressions of how faith and life continue to be connected, from people of all ages and throughout the area parishes.

Because we are in a rather unique situation with five parishes working together, synchronizing our liturgies is an easy tool for evangelism. We have an area Mass schedule, so that throughout the cluster masses are offered at different times, giving people a choice of many times to attend Mass. We gather together the liturgy committees of each of the parishes to do our seasonal liturgy planning. Such gatherings include prayer, some in-service or educational input, music, and group planning. Then a liturgy community in each parish of the cluster incorporates the common elements of this plan into their parish. We have initiated an area music program to ensure that the same hymns are sung throughout the cluster each week. In that way, if someone wishes to go to a different parish, he or she will feel welcomed and a part of that community as well.

Evangelizing isn't that difficult. It is a matter of being a friend or neighbor. It's a matter of using common sense ways to connect ordinary life with faith. It's a matter of doing what seems right, right then.

Sanctifying the Neighborhood:

INSERTING A CHURCH INTO THE COMMUNITY

REVEREND MARK BECKWITH, rector
All Saints Episcopal Church, Worcester, MA

When I arrived in Worcester, Massachusetts, eight years ago, I found a church somewhat confused as to where it was and where it should go. This Episcopal congregation, which was known as the church of the landed gentry thirty years ago, was now in the middle of a poor Hispanic neighborhood, and most of the church members had moved into the outer rings of the city or into the suburbs. I realized that one of my biggest tasks was to help this church connect to a surrounding neighborhood that over the years had become very different from the congregation.

Worcester is a city of 170,000, and for years it has lived in the shadow of Boston, an hour to the east. It has long had a lack of self-esteem because it is a mid-sized sort of rust-belt city that had its heyday forty or fifty years ago. It still has a strong tax base and a stable population, but it seems to lack direction, as did All Saints Episcopal Church, a beautiful gothic building with a wonderful worship space. When you see the church from the outside, you get the sense that you need a secret handshake to get in, or a special pass that indicates that you are a proper Episcopalian. It had a reputation, although not deserved, for being a citadel of the elite. My sense was that it *seemed* exclusive and isolated from the neighborhood around it.

One of our first significant opportunities to interact with our neighborhood was a tragic one. In September 1993, a drug deal about two blocks away from the church ended in murder. Although it did not involve people who lived in that immediate area, it terrorized everyone in the neighborhood. Several of us in the congregation decided that we needed to respond, but we had no idea how. Should we call City Hall? Do we show up somewhere? We pondered and we prayed.

What we do best at All Saints Episcopal is worship, so we designed a liturgy using prayer and water, song and cross, and we marched through the neighborhood to reconsecrate the ground. We invited the people in the neighborhood to come along with us. About a hundred people in the neighborhood joined us. This liturgy helped to make the neighborhood feel safer because the presence of God had been brought into the neighborhood after an event that seemed to expel Him. We marched a second time, with the same number of people, and then a third. We marched with members of a Jewish temple who wanted to go with us. We carried the Star of David and the Cross, we sang inclusive hymns, and we sprinkled water, a sign that held significance for both the Jewish and Christian tradition. It was a wonderful action for us to take together, Jews and Christians, consecrating the ground, bringing our common witness into the community.

But the marches did not go forward without some feelings of awkwardness regarding our obvious differences from the neighborhood residents. We didn't know these people whose neighborhood we were marching through, and they didn't know us. They saw our female priest marching, and I imagine they thought, "What the heck is that?" They could not figure any of this out. We realized that marching wasn't enough—we needed to get to know our neighborhood. We stopped marching and started looking for new ways to connect.

One way we developed a connection was through an after-school program with kids from the neighborhood. At the local soup kitchen, we started helping kids with their homework, then moved to our church and began a daily routine of crafts, games, and study. After several years we defined this as a Christian ministry, and we introduced Bible study. Through these children, we met their parents and began building up some trust, a slow and fragile task, as this was trust that could be lost in the blink of an eye. But nevertheless, we developed relationships with a lot of kids. Several years later, there was a drive-by shooting in a housing complex about four blocks from the church; again, a drug deal not involving anyone who lived in the complex. But, again, the families were terrified.

This time our response could be different. Many of the kids in our after-school program lived in this complex. We thought and prayed about our response. We began prayer meetings on Friday nights from nine to eleven, gathering together with people in the housing complex. With them, we designed a liturgy using English and Spanish prayers and songs, and candles. We invited the police, we held hands and sang, once again reconsecrating the ground and creating a feeling of solidarity—that evil was not the only presence in this neighborhood. We had several of these services, and we developed more relationships and fostered more allegiances of trust with our neighbors.

But then, as a congregation, we wondered if all we were called to do was respond to crises in our neighborhood. We decided that we needed to have an ongoing connection with the neighborhood, to have a fluidity between the people who attended church and those who lived around it. Indeed, we were already bringing some people from the neighborhood into the church. If they were not coming to worship, they were at least coming to our dinners and concerts. We needed to figure out how to develop a ministry in the neighborhood and not just be present when there was crisis or tragedy. We looked to a model in Sheffield, England, called the Urban Theological Unit (UTU), which was founded by John Vincent, a Methodist pastor, who for several decades has sought to engage gospel and neighborhood in a new and different way. In England, except for the noted Cathedrals and isolated vibrant congregations, the church seems to be moribund. In England's cities, this problem is particularly troublesome. Much of the churches' decline has to do with the fact that urban populations are now 40 to 50 percent Muslim. It is not the intention of the UTU to try and convert Muslims to Christianity—but there is a deep need to be in relationship with one another.

Central to the UTU model is a rigorous reading of the Gospel of Mark, which we read for the purpose of helping us discern our ministry in the neighborhood. Similar to the process of "African" Bible study, we reflected on what the text was saying to first-century disciples, what it is saying to us today, and how it was challenging us to engage with the neighborhood.

We then did a systematic study of the demographics of the neighborhood, trying to get a sense of who

these people are. We purchased "Precept" data—
which provided a raft of demographic, economic, and
sociological data from census material for our immediate neighborhood. On the basis of this, we built a
core purpose and some core values, and two sum-
mers ago we developed a new strategy of ministry,
which was committed to continuing an ongoing
presence *in* the neighborhood along with an institutional commitment *to* the neighborhood.

About ten or fifteen people from All Saints began
walking the neighborhood once a week, every
Wednesday night for an hour and a half, meeting
people. We had several routes. We met people, found
out who they were. (A scene from one of these walks
is featured in the documentary film *A Spirit in the
Land: The Transforming Power of Local Churches,* available
through the Pastoral Summit at www.pastoralsummit.
org.) We asked them if they knew who we were. We
always felt good if they did, but we were a bit embarrassed if they did not. We asked how we could pray
for them, and the requests were usually for healing of
a family member for a troublesome issue in the neighborhood. We brought those prayers into our worship
during the prayers of the people.

But developing this ministry did not come without
tension in the congregation. We developed an arts
and crafts and games program in the neighborhood
behind a pharmacy. When the summer ended, we
went Christmas caroling through the neighborhood,
and at Easter we hosted an egg hunt. We did anything

we could think of. Some folks in the congregation said that we needed to do more, that we needed to move faster, that we needed to buy a place in the neighborhood and establish a permanent ministry there. Others argued that we needed to think this through a little more and develop more relationships and base our ministry in the church. We are still not absolutely clear about what our next steps should be for our congregation's health and the health of the neighborhood, but we know we need to continue to be in relationship, whatever form that might take. It's confusing, it's upsetting, it's frustrating, and it's exhilarating.

But through all this, God is clearly showing us a way to be and challenging us to develop a certain "habit of being." We are discovering that when a Yankee congregation engages with a predominantly Hispanic neighborhood, there is mutual conversation. Horizons expand. Unnamed cultural and ethnic assumptions (and prejudices) rise to the surface. We are discovering where and how else God is working. We are learning from this, and we are being converted.

Through this ministry, we have begun to better understand our role in this neighborhood. We have been a congregation since 1835 and on our present site since 1879, making us one of the most concrete presences in the neighborhood. This stability is something we can offer to a neighborhood that is, demographically and economically, very unstable. The local school has a 75 percent annual turnover—meaning that 75 percent of the kids who go to school there are not there the next year.

This ministry is very much a work in progress. We don't have the answers. We have lots of questions, and sometimes we do not have as much clarity as we would like. Nevertheless, by virtue of who we are and where we are, we feel called to continue this mission, to continue this journey with our members and with other congregations—to continue to involve ourselves in the mystery of God working in the midst of this community.

Evangelizing the Marginalized— and Ourselves

VALERIE CHAPMAN, pastoral administrator
St. Francis of Assisi, Portland, OR

One day, a man named Bob, who had been living on the streets and under the bridges of Portland, told me he wanted to know more about the church. He had been attending on and off for eight or nine years, and he had been a regular guest in our dining hall, which serves meals to homeless people, new immigrants, the indigent, and the poor. That day I encouraged Bob to join our Rite of Christian Initiation for Adults (RCIA) classes, which all people who want to become Catholics attend. RCIA classes come with a lot of handouts about the faith, about Catholic practices, about our social teachings. But Bob couldn't read.

And when Bob began to take those classes to some-day join St. Francis of Assisi as a full-fledged member, everything I did as a minister was called into question, everything I believed about how to do social ministry had to change.

As Catholics, we had always heard that we need to be disciples, to model Jesus' ministry in what we do and say to other people. Without much preparation time, this principle had to be put into practice: One member of the group couldn't read, and another was a professor who taught teachers how to teach students to read. There was no way I could rely on the old standby handouts: The differences were too great. In the mix something began to happen on several different levels. The catechists had to be prepared to talk about their faith. The learners had to be patient with one another, with all of us respecting the other's gifts and limita-tions, and quietly, without the rest of the group know-ing, the professor began teaching Bob to read.

Bob attended all the classes faithfully. He listened attentively and at first only spoke when directly asked a question. As the year progressed and he began to feel more comfortable, he ventured to share his own story and his faith with others in the group. His stories of being raised in the Pennsylvania backwoods, of learning to make moonshine with his dad, of traveling across the country by rail were always interesting. His faith was simple and direct. He liked St. Francis Parish because the people did something, not just talked about it. He wanted that faith.

As Easter approached, and our new RCIA class was to "graduate" and become Catholics and members of the parish, the St. Francis community had to take seriously the tough issue of what it meant to have someone who was homeless actually join our church. The Pastoral Council began to officially discuss the issue. Do we baptize this person, and then tell him "Good bye and good luck! Keep warm and well fed?" Or does the Gospel call us to do something more radical, like invite him in? And if we give him a place to stay, what will that be like? After living outside for years, will he even know how to take care of his space? Could we, would we, take the risk?

Each year during Holy Week the candidates and sponsors all gather for a Seder meal. When we gathered that year at our Seder meal, everyone in turn read a part of the service. When it came to be Bob's turn he did not pass as usual, instead, he read, and we cried. When Bob came out dressed in his long white robe, with shaggy long hair, his long beard and sandals to be baptized at our pre-dawn Easter service, there was a quiet hush. Bob was immersed, and as he rose from the water the assembly spontaneously rose to their feet. We have never recovered.

Bob had no place to live, and we had a huge former rectory—which is now our parish offices—so we had to face the fact that we had something that someone in our midst needed: a home. Fast-forward five years—Bob has been living in the former rectory since he joined the church. He is our nighttime caretaker.

I have learned about ministry to the marginalized, embracing that term in all its complexity, by being with the marginalized, by being with people like Bob. As the parish has begun to spend time with those who are homeless, the poor, and the immigrants and to hear their stories, we have begun to realize that they have as much to teach us as we do them. And gradually "us and them" have blended into "we."

In an even broader sense, I think of my entire parish community as marginal—marginally on the edge of Catholicism. We are the parish people come to when they feel they might not be welcome in other Catholic parishes. We are often the first stop back for many recovering Catholics. On any given Sunday eight to twelve former priests are part of the congregation. There are a large number of gay and lesbian people who are a part of the congregation. We have people who are poor, we have recent immigrants, and we have a substantial middle class element. Although the parish is predominantly Anglo, we have a small but growing number of Hispanics, mostly from the dining hall community, and a handful of other ethnic minorities. About 50 to 60 percent of the community is middle class professional—mostly social service people with only a few upper-middle class folks, a large group of working-class households, and 10 to 15 percent very poor.

We find common ground for ministering to this wide array of people by basing our church mission on the discipline of hospitality. This means you must respect each person, whoever they are, whatever their faith, and whatever gifts or deficits they might have. This can be especially challenging in the neighborhood our church is in. Half of our parish is bounded by a light industrial district. The other half is an aging but up-and-coming residential area. Many of the older homes are divided into apartments. There are people who live in the industrial area as well, but they live in old hotels, apartments over businesses, in shelters (there are three within our boundaries), or under the bridges—the parish western boundary is the river, and we have four bridges there. The people in the residential neighborhood do not like to claim the industrial area folks as part of their neighborhood.

We have blended the two divergent communities in our parish-run dining hall, which has been a ministry of St. Francis for almost twenty-two years. Without the dining hall, we would not be the parish we have become. Our vision is to build a community there, to cross the lines that divide us, be they racial, socioeconomic, or ethnic. The St. Francis community is made up of the three hundred people who worship with us on Sunday, the three hundred who eat at the dining hall six days a week, and the people who come by day to St. Francis of Assisi Park.

The park community is diverse, including some ordinary neighborhood folks who come to spend some time, but, by and large, includes a more transient clientele looking for a safe place to sit for a while without being harassed or told to move on. Many of the "housed" neighbors find the regular park people undesirable. With some effort, the parish has held on to its mission of hospitality and welcomes all who are able to follow the minimal rules. We provide portable toilets and a place to keep shopping carts or bicycles so that the park is not cluttered, and we provide a security presence at peak use times in the year.

We've used several methods to pull our many communities together. When we took over the dining hall, we got rid of the long institutional tables and put in round tables to encourage discussion and get more people talking face-to-face. We invited people from our worship community to be part of the dining hall community, and vice versa. Of the three hundred people in the worship community, the number of people who volunteer is high—35 to 40 percent are involved with something. In the dining hall people can help with meal preparation, set up, and serving. They can volunteer to help with art classes, chess tournaments, or soccer games. There is work to maintain the twice-weekly showers, to keep the grounds picked up, and to assist with the county health clinic. We also encourage people to just come and get to know people. Sit down. Have some coffee and conversation.

When people are involved in ministry they take ownership and help shape what happens. This high level of individual commitment to social justice allows our congregation to take risks. When we celebrated our 125th anniversary we had breakfast after the Mass with the whole community—the dining hall community and the worshipping community and special guests and the archbishop—all in one room, undivided, and it worked. When we have parish social events, we open our doors and invite the poor to come in too. Members of the community regularly invite some of our poorest members home to supper or out for coffee. We have learned about addictions and mental illness, and we have learned to not be afraid.

The dining hall opens Monday through Friday at 10 A.M. People can come in, use the phones, bathrooms, and lockers; check the bulletin board; drink coffee; and sit for a while. If the weather is nice the hall closes again at 11:30 A.M. so that the staff and volunteers can begin meal preparation that includes lunch for those who volunteer at the hall and would not otherwise have lunch. At 1:00 P.M. lunch is served, and at 1:30 P.M. the doors are opened for general community for the rest of the day. This is when people can participate in activities or services or play cards, read and talk with friends, all while remaining warm and dry. Since 1996 we have always had at least one Spanish-speaking, preferably Hispanic, staff member. Before that time there was considerable racial tension between the immigrant community and the largely Anglo street community. At this time all of the assistants as well as the director speak fluent Spanish. As a result, the two groups cooperate, and we have a much better volunteer rate among the Hispanic community than existed before we had Spanish-speaking staff.

Managing homeless people's personal possessions is always difficult. We provide some locker space, but there is always a waiting list. Many people have shopping carts filled with belongings, so we provide a space for shopping cart parking. But often people leave their things behind when they move on, either by choice or because they become inpatients in the correction system or another institution for a time. We try to keep their goods as long as possible, but stuff accumulates and "taking"—theft—is a way of survival for some. We are learning to be good at conflict resolution.

Financing the dining hall is a major project in itself, but we have used and built on some existing resources to do it. When we took total responsibility of the dining hall, we began slowly to build a mailing list that now has about eight thousand names. These financers, who donate anywhere from $2 to $5,000, come from all denominations and business groups. We also hold a fund-raising auction on the Tuesday night before Ash Wednesday—Mardi Gras—complete with live music, great food, lots of costumes, and fantastic items to bid on. This auction gathers people from outside the parish as well as inside to help raise $35,000 to $40,000 for operating costs and at the same time gets the message out about St. Francis Dining Hall.

We have a commitment to just wages and that means paying staff justly. The highest cost for the dining hall has always been personnel—currently there are one part-time cook, one back-up cook, two assistants to the director, and the director. The annual budget of the dining hall is more than $289,000 a year, but we have never been short.

Operating the dining hall has radically changed our worshipping community. As we began to listen to the stories of the people who come to eat, we discovered that people in these other communities have something to teach us. We deal with people who are drug addicts, mentally ill, recently out of prison, developmentally delayed, new immigrants, and others, and they teach us something every single day.

For example, there are many undocumented immigrants. In hearing stories of life in their countries, I was forced to learn about politics and the resulting effect on the indigenous people of our hemisphere. I shared my learning with the parish, and we began to make a connection with a community living high in the hills of Guatemala. Eventually I went to study Spanish in Mexico and then went on to Guatemala, to the village we were communicating with. I hand-delivered a gift of money from the parish to a Mayan single mothers' group living far away from many of the conveniences of the modern world. The money was a tithe from a generous gift the parish had received. In the village I met women whose husbands, brothers, or sons were living in the United States earning money to send back home.

I have learned that drug-addicted people are not bad people, regardless of the drugs they do. They are only sick people struggling to live each day without much hope for recovery or kindness in the process. I have learned not to take good mental health for granted, and I have learned that mentally ill people are real people with real feelings and real needs, hopes, and dreams. I have learned how poorly we as a society prioritize our money, often cutting such important services as drug and alcohol treatment facilities, clean and sober housing, and mental health care. I have learned not to give up trying even when the system is broken because people, all people, matter.

If we want to live healthy and holy lives, we can learn from one another. It makes me consider how the way I live—do I have more than my share of this society's resources?—affects the people who come to the dining hall community and how the way they live, with very few of their basic needs met, affects me. I wonder, "Can we be in this together?" At St. Francis we have found that when we change, in both our thinking and our actions, people begin to ask us about our faith. We preach with what we do and hope that we do not use too many words.

Practicing hospitality on large and small scales has changed our community. We strive to accept and welcome people right where they are, to listen to their stories, to treat them kindly and with respect. We are fueled by small victories, as we see the fruits of our attempts. Sam, a man who never spoke, is one of those small triumphs. When I first met him, he slept in the bark dust by the side of the church where dogs are often tethered. He didn't smell good. No one knew if he could talk. He wore a number of shabby coats, even in the summer. He was a stereotypical example of the "marginalized."

I continued to welcome Sam and invite him in. I always spoke to him as if he could talk. Then early one Sunday morning out of the blue he looked at me and said, "Good morning, Valerie." I was stunned and for some reason immediately thought of that passage in Isaiah "I have called you by name...." I believe we meet God in the marginalized. I hope and pray that we can be Christ for them as well.

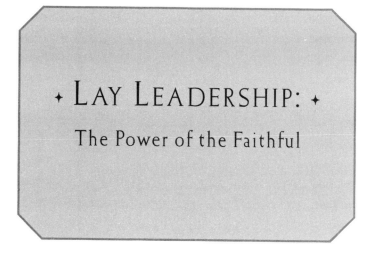

✦ LAY LEADERSHIP: ✦
The Power of the Faithful

Making Disciples—
Then What?

TRAINING FOR THE NEWLY
INVOLVED/CONVERTED

MONSIGNOR ARTURO BAÑUELAS, pastor
St. Pius X, El Paso, TX

St. Pius X is a predominately middle-class bilingual community of more than 2,700 families. We are grounded both in the vision of Vatican II and the religious heritage of the Mexican-American border culture. As for staff, we have a deacon who operates a business in a nearby shopping mall, a part-time director of religious education, a part-time evangelization director, and myself. In addition to being pastor, I am the director of the Tepeyac Institute, which is a lay training institute. With that many parishioners and that small a staff, it is obvious we need a tremendous amount of lay involvement if we are to be effective and to meet both the parish needs and the needs of our city, El Paso, and those of Juarez, which adjoins us, across the Mexican border.

Within our parish, more than seven hundred men and women have been trained in ministry in the last ten years. Hundreds more are active. This just does not happen by coincidence, and it does not happen without planning and excellent training. We ask everyone in our parish who is in ministry, or expresses a desire to be in ministry, to go through a basic formulation program at Tepeyac Institute here in El Paso. (See www.elpasodiocese.org/tei for more information about the Tepeyac Institute.) They study theology, Christology, Vatican II, and the Church's social documents. As virtually all of the students are employed, Tepeyac classes are offered in the evenings, on weekends, and during the summer. We must make it possible for the average person to attend. After this, they go though an evangelization retreat.

These are the two key aspects of those who want to be in ministry in the parish. Tepeyac gives theology and spiritual formation so that everybody has a sense of common vision and language to speak of their experience with God, church, and their ministry. Again, this is grounded on the Mestizo cultural heritage of the border as well the directives of Vatican II, which called for a new vision of the Church and a new vision of the priesthood of all believers.

The evangelization retreat gives people a sense of an encounter with the Lord and community. It is more personal. But our training doesn't end there. There is ongoing training at the parish, an annual retreat, and opportunities for reflection. Preaching in the parish and all the missions throughout the year are geared toward the same thrust that the ministers get in the training.

In the summer, we have additional, advanced programs at Tepeyac. People from all over the country conduct the programs and give in-depth formation to the people who have already had their initial formation at the Institute. We do other things like an insert in the bulletin once a month for Catholic updating. It is required that if you are in a ministry you must do ongoing theological formation, participate in a study group, and go through some videos.

But training people for ministry is not just giving them a program. It is about dealing with their assumptions about church, the priest, and their ministry. You can "give" people the sacraments, but they will still have their own notion about what a sacrament will be. You can encourage devotions, but you need to place them in a larger context. We need to address these things. The first thing we address is the shift in the way that our people see church. For most people in our tradition, when you say "Catholic Church" they think of the Pope, bishops, rules, doctrines, and dogmas. These are an important part of the Church, but one of the notions that has worked very powerfully for us is the notion that we are not just anonymous figures within this thing called "the Church," but a community with a mission. We have worked very hard in showing that God's relationship with us is lived out in our relationship with one another and in the gifts that emerge from this. We have worked hard in forming relationships within the community. We have a lot of fiestas, a lot of activities, and a lot of prayer together. It is important for them to see themselves as a community.

The question is often asked: How do you get people to come in and be ministers in the first place? We use all kinds of strategies. We have a ministry fair every year, which is highly attended. But this will not work until the people have a sense that they are a community with a mission and that they own the church. When they start owning it, then it is their responsibility to minister. So you start having a different focus. It then becomes easy to get people. They come up and say, "I want to do something." This will all be very difficult if they do not have a sense that they own the church or have a sense of mission.

Also, we are a parish that is open to anyone's suggestion of what we could do or do better. When Marta Huerta saw an AIDS patient dying without love, she started the Arms of Love AIDS ministry. When Tom Chavez created a Passion drama, he realized this should not only happen at Easter, and so the Living

Word Ministry was created to make the gospels come alive week after week. And although we are grateful for our successes, people know we are willing to experiment and are willing to be fools and sometimes fail.

The other aspect that we address is that people must have a different notion of priest. One of the biggest changes for us was when people saw the shift from being the father's helpers to being father's collaborators. In this, the priest's role is not diminished but takes on a different kind of significance and importance. He will be spiritual mentor, enabler, and facilitator of the community. I have been a priest for twenty-five years, and because of the emergence of lay ministry in the parish, I am probably more excited about being a priest today then when I was ordained. The parish provides seminary training for lay people, and this has renewed my sense of how to work and collaborate with our community. Ministerial growth has shifted. They are not there to help me. It's their church. We ask: "What is their gift? What is their ministry? And how do we work together?" We have forty-three ministries, and each one is present at every council gathering. I sometimes get outvoted. We see ourselves as collaborating, and father is not always right. Still, the leadership role of the priest is very important in our community.

Another crucial aspect is that of parishioners seeing themselves as ministers: that training people for ministry is not just offering them a couple of courses and bringing them back to the parish and putting them to work. We are dealing with some basic assumptions of who they are as ministers and that there has been an explosive shift in their lives. When they shift their understanding that they are not volunteers in the church, but really called by their baptism to be ministers, this takes on a dignity of being about God's work among us. Each one has that dignity. And so, we never use the word "volunteer." It is a nasty word for ministers and does not respect their baptismal call.

The next thing that is very important to stress is that there is only one priest, and that is Jesus. Jesus manifests himself in many different ways in the community, according to the different gifts. The more gifts we have, the more present Jesus is and we are, in turn, more present to one another. This notion that father does everything is gone. They realize that the priest does not have all the gifts. The Holy Spirit is the architect of all the gifts in the church. The church has all the gifts it needs to do the work of the kingdom. We need to facilitate and bring their gifts together.

There are other issues. We struggle with what to call people. "Lay minister" has a negative connotation. Nevertheless, it is very important to promote that they are baptized, and though their baptism they are anointed to participate in the priesthood of Jesus Christ and in his mission to build his kingdom. They are not there to become lay people or be initiated into a second-class status in the church.

In all of this, we have to realize that people have lives, they have jobs, and they received or did not receive good Christian education. And so we have to train people with the realities of where they are. We cannot just import some fancy seminary curriculum—as good as it might be—for it will have no context of the community. The cultural symbols, the language, all have to be taken into consideration when you train people. What is our context, what is our reality? When you bring this up and touch it to people's lives, it is explosive.

We have many ministries at St. Pius X, and I think it is very important that the parish have installation celebrations to recognize the people who are in ministry. I am speaking of the people who are not paid, not the salaried ministers. You need to recognize officially before the community the gifts that people have, the ministry to which they feel called, the ministry the community as a whole sanctions, blesses, and supports. There are very few places in the church to do this. A liturgy before the community, a certificate—these are visible signs of their being ordained to perform a ministry.

Having trained lay ministers in our community is one of the fundamental reasons our parish is so strong and so alive today. God has blessed us with tremendous gifts in our parish with these ministers. In fact, we could not exist without them. We would not exist without them.

The Care and
Training of
Lay Leaders

+

DAWN MAYER, pastoral associate
and director of family faith and life
Holy Family Parish, Inverness, IL,
Church of the Holy Spirit, Schaumburg, IL

I work at two parishes in the Archdiocese of
Chicago. Holy Family Parish in Inverness,
Illinois, is a very large community, 3,700 fami-
lies, in the somewhat affluent northwest suburbs of
Chicago. We are located in the shadow of Willow
Creek Community Church and have, at times,
looked to Willow Creek for ideas and strategies
on caring for the large number of volunteer

ministers they have involved. I also work at Church of the Holy Sprit in Schaumburg, which is a bit smaller, about 2,600 families, but it is a parish of great multicultural diversity. We have a large and growing Hispanic population. Our 12:30 P.M. Mass, our largest, is in Spanish. We have a significant number of Filipino families as well as a growing number of families from India and Africa. We have quite a large number of people who are relatively new to the parish (and the country) and a large number of people who have been there since the parish was founded almost thirty years ago. As seemingly different as they are, both parishes operate on a renewed ecclesiology, which calls for a new kind of leader.

Catholic tradition operates on a vertical model of church that we are all familiar with. There are the pope, cardinals, bishops, priests, deacons, masters degree people who work in the church, trained lay people, and then, at the bottom of the pyramid, there are the people of God. Often the people at the bottom of that pyramid have been accustomed to the church "giving" them the sacraments and some religious education, baptizing them, marrying them, and burying their loved ones.

At Holy Family and Church of the Holy Spirit, we continue to try to move from this understanding of church to a renewed ecclesiology with Jesus as the center of our life and ministry and different people sharing their gifts and talents along with those called to leadership and service, giving order to that chaotic mess.

When we remember the story of the early Church in the Acts of the Apostles, we recall they did not have everything neatly outlined and diagrammed and charted out. It's a Church that was kind of messy. People were going in all kinds of directions. Somehow those early disciples needed to give vision, inspire passion, and try to pull all these folks together. I believe that part of what ministry is about today is really encouraging the gifts of the Spirit that are present within each person, not just following a model or a program that's been done somewhere else. Ministry at Holy Family and at Church of the Holy Spirit can, at times, be very messy. In the chaos, and what at times appears to be a "mess," the Spirit is very much present and active, and the mission of the reign of God does emerge.

Another thing we try to do is encourage our people to really see themselves as the "priesthood of the faithful"—not by virtue of ordination, but by the call of our baptism we are sent to serve. Each person in our assembly, each person in our worshipping community, each person registered or bumping into us in whatever way, shape, or form is called to serve the people of God. How that looks in any individual person's life is the journey of a lifetime. At Holy Family we have a highly developed process called "Gifted" that seeks to help discern the gifts and charisms of each person and how they can be used for ministry. When we call for leaders, we do not just say announce: "We need 232 catechists. Please come over and sign up." We are very much against using the *"Price is Right*...come-on-down" approach. We engage people in a process. We ask them to seriously reflect on what they believe their gifts and talents are. We encourage them to check that out with other people. Sometimes people have a gift they don't even know they have. Then we ask them to reflect on what are the needs of the parish community at this time and how their gifts match those needs. Sometimes to get a program off the ground we try to fill slots, but filling slots in the long run really does not work. We need to match gifts and needs. Occasionally we come across people or talents that there is no niche for, which can be the Holy Sprit saying: "You have not thought of everything that is needed. Someone still has a gift to share!"

Another principle we operate out of is the model of Servant Leadership. This is not about a power- or ego-trip. This can happen within churches as it happens in all institutions. Although we certainly have people who are responsible for huge areas of ministy, we believe in the model of ministry that Jesus gave us when he got on his knees, put a towel around his waist, and washed his disciples' feet. Ministry is not always glamorous; it is sometimes about making the coffee and putting out the doughnuts and cleaning up the place. I believe that as people see us as servant leaders, they themselves understand what it is to be a servant leader.

Another key principle is Faith First. Every parish meeting—large and small, staff or laity—starts not just with prayer or scripture but also specifically with the proclamation of the upcoming Sunday Gospel.

When I came to Holy Family about eight years ago, I began to wonder if hearing the Sunday Gospel every day, sometimes three times a day as we have a lot of meetings, was going to make an impact. But this practice of Faith First has transformed that community of faith. When the parish gathers on Sunday and hears the Word broken open, it is with numbers of people, including teens and children, who have been meeting and praying over the Gospel all during the week. I believe as the Gospel is read, our assembly is allowing that Word to transform us in ways that we could have never imagined.

Holy Family Parish and Church of the Holy Spirit are parishes with great creativity. It is important for us to "think outside the box." It's not that we do things differently just for the sake of being different, but because we have found that our people and our lives have changed and some things simply don't work anymore. For example, the naming of programs at Holy Family helps reflect the intention of the program or service. Footsteps in Faith is for the journey toward Christian Initiation. FAITH is an acronym that stands for Faith Alive in the Home, our religious education program for children and families that tries to emphasize that faith must be alive not just in the home of the catechist, but also in all the homes of the parish. Foundations is our adult education program that addresses the core of who we are as a Catholic people with Search for God, Search for Jesus, and Search for Community. EPIC is the name of our young adult

ministry. Everything has a name. Besides giving identity to a program, it makes it much more interesting
when people are trying to ask about a program. And,
it really speaks to the creativity of the people.

As the ministries of Holy Family continued to grow,
there was a downside to all this activity. We have more
than 120 ministries going in many different directions, and we realized that there was no sense of being
harnessed any place in the center. So about six years
ago, we began the development of what we call our
Leadership Community structure. On the second
Tuesday of every month the leadership of the parish
gathers together. These are the leaders of all the ministries that operate in the parish community, which
are in turn divided into eight specific ministering
communities. Every first Tuesday of the month, more
than one hundred people gather to hear the
announcements that impact the whole parish, individual community reports, and dialogue about the "business" of the parish. Here is the way we have divided
our ministries:

Operation Ministries—The finance committee and
the nuts and bolts of making the parish run.

Communications Ministry—We have an extensive
web site with more than 250 places to visit. We just
added "streaming," where people can click onto the
latest homily, a reflection on the Stations of the Cross,
a history of the Cross of New Life, or topics that
appeal to teens and young adults. We have a parish
bulletin that is 24 pages long every week and is

mailed to our parishioners once a month. We have a parish newspaper, which is inserted into the *Chicago Tribune* twice a year in our area. When folks open their paper, among the ads and comics, they find the Holy Family newspaper. It's another way to evangelize and to get the message out. Tapping into the way people take in information is key. We must be much more aware these days of how our parishioners communicate. I have a four-year-old daughter who can maneuver a mouse and get onto a computer. We have to be able to communicate in a way that especially our children and young people can understand. We are working with our Internet Ministry to create interactive pages that contain information for parents, teens, and children.

Adult Formation Ministry—Many of our adult formation ministries are based on a needs survey that the parish did some months ago. We are not just offering programs for the sake of asking, "Wouldn't it be great to get together and talk about whatever?" but rather what people are dealing with: depression, stress, parenting their children, having an aging parent at home. We try to tap into people's lives and develop programs that are church-based, yet very practical. We have found people flock to them because of this unique combination of the religious and the practical.

Neighborhood Ministry—The New Image of Parish is our movement toward neighborhood ministry. In a world where people sometimes don't even talk to the person who lives next door, our neighborhood ministry tries to create neighborhood areas where ministry can happen, not just at the central place of Holy Family. Our neighborhood ministers welcome newcomers, set up our small faith-sharing groups according to neighborhoods, and gather folks together at a Sunday Mass followed by social time. This past year neighborhood groups were invited to fish fries on Friday nights followed by the Stations of the Cross. We averaged between 200 and 250 each Friday night! Our goal is to create a Sunday experience that is a cathedral experience where all these small groups of the parish come together. We also have a men's ministry, women's ministry, and a group of families that participates in the Christian Family Movement.

The area that I am responsible for is Family Faith and Life. We have a deep investment in the faith formation of our children and our families. We have more than 1,500 children in our religious education programs and 350 catechists that lead small groups that meet all over the parish and neighborhood. We are committed to helping parents be the first and best religious educators of their children. As we continue to offer programs, we have begun to realize that we have many people who may not have the language or the skills, but they have the desire—along with a good dose of fear—to pass on faith to their children.

We did an evening where we had our sixth graders take a "road rally" through the parish and "visit" the different places of the Bible. The kids were running all over the place, asking their parents to help them find the next clue. At each of the "stops" they had to look up a passage in the Bible to find the answer to the puzzle. Many of our parents felt embarrassed that they did not know how to look things up. What are we thinking? We are assuming that people have the vocabulary, that they have to tools to communicate faith to their children. In many cases it is not a question of why didn't they get it, but rather that some of us didn't teach it to them. We need to start there, with parents and their kids together, and go from there. We have to help them walk with God as they venture into faith formation with their children.

Youth Ministry—We continue to develop a program that has an evangelical outreach to the young people of our parish. Our Youth Ministry programs reflect the "fire" that we hope is burning in the hearts of our youth. Our programs are called Ignite, Flame, and Torch. Ignite is gathering the group that is targeted toward outreach. Teens of the parish and beyond are invited on a monthly basis to a night of fun with a message that is geared toward teen issues. Flame is the religious education dimension of the program, giving kids the tools to understand Catholicism and the foundations of our faith. Torch is our name for social events and fun activities, and Celebrating the Spirit is the Confirmation preparation program where we help teens name their gifts and then encourage them to minister to the community and beyond.

Pastoral Care Ministry—This ministering community works on reaching people at times of need. We offer a number of support groups and twelve-step groups, and we have many people trained to work with families who have experienced a loss in the planning of the funeral liturgy. We also have Ministers of Care who visit the sick and the shut-in. The parish is blessed to have a parish nurse who assists in these ministries.

Outreach and Justice Ministry—Every year Holy Family adopts a theme for the year. We try to support causes locally like our PADS (Public Action to Deliver Shelter), and we have some international ministries in Belize and Guatemala. Parishioners are sent from the parish on a regular basis to visit our sister parishes in these countries, and they bring with them the gifts of the parish. Sometimes it is much needed medical supplies, other times cards and letters from our First Communicants to their First Communicants.

Worship Ministry—This group is responsible for anything having to do with our worship, which is a huge responsibility.

The training of our servant leaders is key to our Leadership Communities. We train leaders in a very specific ministry style. We have determined we cannot be in the "do for" ministry. Rather, our work as staff people is to train and work with a group of leaders who target a ministry population. Every ministry is owned by the people of God, not just one particular staff member. Our structures are designed so that as people's lives change, staff people change, and all sorts of things change, that ministry can continue above and beyond the work of any one person. Our

Pastoral Council is made up of a member from all eight leadership communities plus four others "at large" who monitor rhythm of the parish.

I've learned a lot from the success and failures of my work as a layperson within a parish, but one of the key things is the importance of checking in. We go off on what began as a good idea and, being so busy in our work and our lives, we forget to check in with the people we work with and the people we are trying to serve. We need to pay attention to the rhythm of people's lives, not just to what the calendar says or how programs worked in the past.

I think it is important that when we call people to leadership in ministry that we give them a clear job description, we invite them to start, and we let them know when they end. This is a lesson we learned in small Christian communities. If is helpful for people to have a beginning and ending time for things when they are getting started. For a first-time small-group experience, folks report, "I can do this for six weeks." If you don't provide an ending time, sometimes you get those looks from people when they think that saying yes means they're in this until they move three states away. Let people say no and leave a group or ministry gracefully. We may be good at getting people to sign on, but I think sometimes we do not help people to exit—when they should, when they need to, when we need them to.

It is important that the assembly acknowledges our leadership. When I started as a youth minister at

Church of the Holy Sprit. I was short and blonde and no one knew who I was. The pastor at the time stood me up in front of the congregation and said, "This is your new youth minister and she is going to say something." He had me speak to the assembly on a regular basis, and they got to know me. I think we need to tell our leadership that it is important for them to stand up in front of the assembly so that people know that right now that person is called to leadership. We need this occasion to be ritualized.

I cannot underscore enough the importance of evaluation. At Holy Family we do not call it evaluation, we call it "re-imagining." The term "evaluation" causes people to groan, but when Father Pat Brennan announces "re-imagining," people are excited. It is important to look at what worked well and what we need to do differently. It's good to have those opportunities where we spend some time just thinking about what *could* be. When we go on staff retreat we ask: "Where do we need to go? What do we need to be planning for? How can we 're-imagine' things that may not have gone as planned?"

If you want a church where many people are really involved, it is important that we make it easy for people to volunteer. People at Holy Sprit and Holy Family are incredibly busy. I have kids with day planners and Palm Pilots. We have people who are so busy trying to do all this stuff that sometimes to volunteer or to see themselves called to ministry is just one more thing that they can't possibly see themselves doing. We have to be aware that if a parent of a young child is going to be doing something, are we going to provide childcare? Is one person in charge of so many things that they are never home? Or can we can we parcel out the ministry, so many people can be involved even if it is just an hour or two here and there? In our religious education program, we started to do that. Rather than having one catechist in charge of one family group, we encourage groups to work together. We have a lead catechist, assistants, and those who can only bake cookies. You say "thank you" and "thank God" for each of them.

We have tried very hard at Holy Family and Church of the Holy Spirit to care for our leaders. We encourage them to grow in their ministry. For a number of years we sent people though the diocese's lay minister training program, but because of the numbers, we couldn't keep sending dozens of people and asking them to drive great distances. So we started our own intensive lay ministry program. Every Tuesday night they meet in prayer, formation and quality adult education on the Bible, the Church, Christology, and other issues related to church life.

Because Holy Family and Church of the Holy Spirit are relatively close together, we try to see if there are ways to do things together; each parish need not see itself as an isolated island. Parishes need to try to work together and share the talents of the different communities.

As mentioned in the Adult Formation Leadership Community, we saw a need for basic, foundational information and so we began the Foundation series. These sessions address the issues that kept coming up from our parish: People wanted a basic understanding of Catholicism. Potential leaders, especially, critically need this. So we have started a Catholicism 101 called Search for God, Search for Jesus, Search for Community. We spend twelve weeks every fall just answering the questions: Where is God? How is God? How do I experience God through other people? Then we spend four or five weeks on Jesus, understanding different aspects of the life, teaching, and ministry of Jesus. In the spring, we offer Search for Community.

Because most people will never attend a seminary or school of theology, it is our vision that the parish is the seminary of the future—in fact, of the present. Many churches have seminaries or schools of theology near them, and they can utilize those resources. Holy Family serves as a satellite site for Dominican University, Loyola, and Chicago Theological Union, so that rather than sending people to the middle of Chicago, we bring the teachers out to the parish. People from many different communities and churches come and take courses at Holy Family.

As we look and reflect on ministries in general, we try to look at our parish needs and goals and ask: "Who are we missing? Whose voice are we missing as we have this conversation?" We need to seek those voices out. We are embarking on this new understanding of parish where a parish is broken into several geographical regions. Each might have needs that the other parts do not. It is important to connect with as many people as possible in the neighborhood, to see ourselves as working within smaller networks within the greater parish. Our size gives us certain advantages, but if we don't see all the "small pictures," the "big picture" will not be as complete as it could be.

Creating a Collaborative Culture

REVEREND PATRICIA FARRIS, senior pastor
First United Methodist Church, Santa Monica, CA

I came to First United Methodist Church, Santa Monica, some four years ago. This is a prestigious, tall-steeple church in the community with a long history of excellent ministries and community involvement. I had been a district superintendent in the United Methodist Church and so had been away from direct pastoral work for a while. But what I had found in my three years as a district superintendent was that more and more churches were turning from a leadership style that many of us had known growing up in the church. As was true of most all large-membership churches through the 1950s to the 1990s, the leadership style was clergy-driven and hierarchical. It relied on the lay participation of a small cohort of faithful souls who had been members of the congregation for years. As a result, there was a rather clearly perceived "in" group of leaders and decision makers while the majority of the congregation was kept on the fringes of information and real leadership.

I knew that I wanted to be a pastor with a much more collaborative style. I dreamed of a church with a shared ministry, a team leadership style in which clergy and laity work together as coequal partners. Many of our members are already experiencing this new management style in their work setting. I wanted to work not with the "in" group or the "out" group, but everyone who came to our doors and wanted to participate in the vision of the church. Perhaps this transformation appears logical, self-evident, or easy. In my experience, it is not.

What the congregation and I had to quickly face together was that our congregation had in fact been in slow but steady decline for approximately four decades. We were large enough and strong enough financially that people really didn't have to pay attention. We also didn't have to think intentionally and systematically about new members, new families, new leadership, finances, or growth. People had assumed that if you lived in this area, were Methodist or some kind of mainline Protestant, you would naturally come to this church. And that leaders naturally presented themselves.

So while the decline was not blamed on me, working a miracle and turning it around was expected of the new senior pastor. There was a real advantage in being new. I began to make some observations much as a visitor might experience. For example, there were no signs anywhere letting people know how to find the restrooms. What had once been assumed knowledge had become a well-kept secret! But as a newcomer, I could in a gentle, loving, and persistent way, invite people to open their eyes and see the situation that we were in. We were not reaching out to the community in the ways that we really needed to. We were too insular and comfortable. Our leadership base was very narrow.

One thing that is crucial as a church begins to take a hard look at itself, the changing religious landscape, and the depth and breadth of its leadership is to create a certain sense of urgency. This is tricky in a large institution that from the outside looks fairly stable and that its members perceive to be solid. None of us trying to help lead change can ever underestimate the magnitude of the forces that reinforce complacency and help maintain the status quo. Inertia is a powerful force, within ourselves as well as our congregants. And the fear of change is always much deeper than we bargain.

Change is not a neat and tidy process. It is not a linear process. I am learning how to gracefully move around people who just cannot seem to embrace it. I can love them, and I will be their pastor, but I cannot let them forever stand in the way of what I think is the movement of the Spirit.

What I keep learning about myself is the importance of my own spiritual life and spiritual care, which is both exhilarating and exhausting. Finding a variety of ways of keeping open to the Spirit while keeping my self centered and flexible is important. Turning around an institution and helping it move in another direction does not happen overnight. I find it tricky to keep the sense of urgency from shifting to a sense of anxiety and fear. I have to work on myself about this. Not to be overtaken by the anxiety and fear is part of the spiritual journey we are on, which is I suppose why it's so central to the Gospel message, because two things are at work simultaneously. One is an eagerness for change. We all want our church to be open and dynamic. But at the same time there is part of us that is afraid of that kind of change and retreats back into the old ways from time to time for a sense of stability. That's in the Bible, too. Remember the people of God journeying to the promised land looking back nostalgically to the slave pots of Egypt!

But what I did discover soon after I got to the church was that many of those long-time members who had been serving on boards and committees were actually tired and ready to have things happen in a new way. They were looking for new people who might share the work and the possibilities of a church with a great history and a real place in our community. I am grateful for God's timing in all of that—I came when they were already at that point. But, still, change is always difficult, regardless of the potential benefits. So, I had to proceed carefully. My work as a district superintendent educated me to the reality that you cannot take a church to places it really doesn't want to go, so part of the leader's challenge is to continually reinforce both the potential benefits of change as well as the dead-ends inherent in refusing to change. One of the great insights of systems management people is their pointing out that a system is already getting results it's designed to get. So, if your results aren't what you want or hope for, you must change how things are being done. We can't simply wish or hope ourselves into a new reality, nor will doing the same things more or better produce different results. We must change our ways of doing things, and that's hard work.

Because there were old leaders who were ready for a break, I quickly found there were many potential new leaders eager to have a say, to have their views solicited, and to have a creative voice in what was going on in the life of the church. Not too far under the surface of the culture of the congregation was a tremendous potential of people wanting to be involved and to serve more.

They were eager, but, equally, they often were rather unsure of their own skills and abilities. It never ceases to amaze me that people who can be competent or skilled in their work setting or homes and neighborhood groups somehow get into the church and feel intimidated by a whole variety of things based on messages they have received over the years—the message that you have to have been a member for so many years, elected to so many committees and of proper standing in the community, or somehow "chosen" or "holy." A big part of my work has been in encouraging people to trust in the gifts and skills they have and to feel comfortable sharing those in the life of the congregation.

We are shifting to a model where clergy and laity are the church together. That's an exciting journey, and I believe that in the midst of that one of a church leader's most important tasks is one of calling and training and empowering.

This is done in a variety of ways. I do a lot of one-on-one meetings with people, a lot of coffee shared, a lot of listening in small groups, trying to create a climate where I know more people, where it is okay for them to say, "I have this idea; how can we do that?" For people to say, "I want to do this—but I do not know how," and, "I do not think I have the skills, but how can I get them?" Out of these sorts of exchanges have come, for example, a group working on the design of new paraments for the sanctuary, another group looking at the graphics of the church's printed materials, and another group rethinking how our small library might be used.

It has also been important to specifically talk with potential leaders about assuming leadership roles in the congregation. I will admit that I blundered into some wonderful choices by talking with people about a leadership role only to discover that they'd never before been asked. I learned to not decide in advance why people weren't serving, not to imagine that they would decline because they were too busy or something and had already been approached many times. Most people are honored to be asked to serve. I think one of our biggest mistakes is in not asking. There are still far too many people who feel left out, unneeded, or unwanted.

I also look for ways to reinforce this one-on-one work through my sermons, teaching, and other larger group settings. For example, I have done a sermon series on "ordinary people—extraordinary lives" looking at a variety of biblical characters who became leaders, often much to their surprise—Esther, Moses, Rahab, Jeremiah, and so forth. It is important to "name" new ways of doing things as people are open to hear and to help give people the larger picture of the change process and its goals.

I am constantly encouraging people—members and staff—to take initiative and try new things, while being very clear that not every great idea pans out. False starts and failure are to be expected. If we are not failing—failing fairly regularly—we are not very alive. We have launched several new small groups and study groups in the last three years that seemed to be just what people were wanting, only to find then that

no one showed up. We've tried some age-level gatherings that never attracted enough people to achieve a
critical mass. It's not stupid to try things that don't
end up working as we thought. But it is stupid to not
take the time to learn as much as we can from the
things that don't work. We need to discipline ourselves to learn from the things that do not work well
and revamp them and do them again in another way.

For example, we have made the transition from
serving communion in the pews to inviting everyone
to come forward to receive. We now have a system
that works fairly smoothly, but to get there we had
to readjust how it worked several times—everything to the kind of bread we used to how large the
pieces are to how to be sure and not miss people
with limited mobility who still needed to be served
in the pew. All this took several months, and along
the way there was a loud clamor to just go back to
the way we had "always done it." Now, a few years
later, people are beginning to experience the joy of
joining together as God's people, coming forward to
receive the gifts of life, and uniting in prayer for one
another as we receive.

I also soon realized that our new emerging leaders
needed training, but when I came to First Church,
there was no budget for any of kind of continuing education for anyone other than the clergy. We have created more study opportunities both within our local
setting to develop and train lay leadership, such as
twice-yearly trainings for lay lectors for the Sunday

morning worship services, and in a series of presentations and small-group experiences to help people identify and live out their own spiritual gifts. There are many workshops in our denomination and ecumenically that we are offering to our people, such as local and regional conferences on youth work, equipping ministries, and worship transformation. We have had to revamp that part of the budget to make some money available for this.

We've created a new leadership configuration within the congregation, and a new, more prayerful approach. Each gathering, each meeting, anytime we came together, we take time for scripture, a time of prayer, and a time of spiritual formation so that all "church work" is seen and experienced as a time of spiritual formation and skill development.

Before meetings and gatherings I work with people to make sure that we have in place what we hope to accomplish in that time. Someone once said that no minute of church work should ever be wasted time. We want our meetings to be times of spiritual growth and significant work. It doesn't always happen, but we are also trying to be intentional about spending time in evaluation. We learn in the church that sometimes we just race on to next thing and do not pause long enough to learn from the experience that we just had to really learn what worked, what didn't, and what we would do differently the next time. We are doing this in each season of the church year in our staff meetings as well as in the meetings of our church council.

I see all of this as ongoing leadership training and development. We have started more groups for spiritual formation and spiritual growth. We have discovered that we do not have the computer software to really track our members and record spiritual gifts as well as other kinds of gifts and talents. We are in the process of researching new software and training our office staff to keep records that will be of more use to us in the future.

In all of this work, I would point out two major cautions I have discovered. First is that these efforts continually need a lot of reinforcement with people. People sometimes get quite excited about this new approach, but then they get stuck or they get tripped up. They go forward a few steps, and then they fall back on old ways either through habit, uncertainty, or just the press of time. I need to keep up with what's going on and keep being with people so they are continually growing in self-confidence in the kinds of things that we are working on. I have also learned to try and remember to expect that this will happen, sometimes when I least expect it or with people I least expect. My own grounding in scripture and in the faithfulness of God to see us through must constantly be fed through prayer and sacrament.

The other caution is that there is a danger of creating a new in-group to replace the old one. People who were quickly responsive my style of leadership, to the way we are working in the church have clustered around, and I think it's important to be intentional about continually expanding the group so that we are always bringing new people into leadership to help train new people.

We used to have an organization within our structure called the nominating committee, and its job was to nominate people to fill classes and slots on already existing committees. That group in our denomination has now been renamed and really rethought. It is now called the Lay Leadership Committee. Its job is to work year-round developing lay leadership and promoting and encouraging training. It is currently working on presenting spiritual gifts to the congregation; on creating small-group settings where people can get to know one another's interests, skills, and gifts; and on enlarging our member data bank.

I am very excited about what all this will enable in terms of shifting our focus from church membership to Christian discipleship. For far too long, the work of the laity has been described as "volunteering" when it really should be understood for what it is—ministry. We are all in ministry together, and the task of the pastor as leader is to empower, inspire, teach, train, and set free. It is also our calling to stay in tune with the leading of the Holy Spirit so that together God's people can give voice and form to the church God would have us to be, in service to the world.

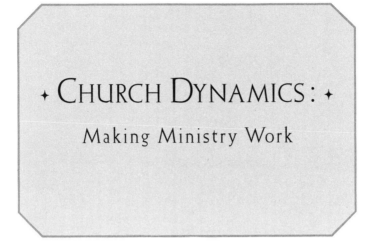

·CHURCH DYNAMICS: ·

Making Ministry Work

Psychological Profile of the Effective Pastor / Lay Minister

FATHER DONALD COZZENS, a priest of the Diocese of Cleveland, is author of *The Changing Face of the Priesthood: A Reflection on the Priest's Crisis of Soul*

Shepherding a parish congregation as pastor or lay ecclesial minister in today's church is arguably as demanding and challenging a ministry as one can find. It's clearly not for the faint of heart. In addition to the regular demands facing priests and pastoral ministers—funerals, weddings, counseling parishioners, and care of the sick and elderly—pastoral leaders must contend with a Catholic world quite different from the halcyon days following World War II. Recent surveys show that most parishioners don't attend Eucharist regularly, and those who take an active role in the life of their parish community continue to dwindle. Add to these realities the progressive-conservative tensions inherent to a postconciliar church, the dramatic decline in the number of ordained priests, not to mention the boundary violations of a significant number of clergy, and an always challenging ministry becomes all the more difficult.

At the same time, vibrant parishes can be found from coast to coast where prayerful worship, a strong sense of community, and social outreach both nourish the spiritual lives of the faithful and proclaim the gospel to their communities and beyond. To a great extent, the vitality of these parishes is due to the pastors and lay ecclesial ministers who provide—often without much recognition or affirmation—vision, leadership, and pastoral care.

I believe we have a good deal to learn from these men and women who shepherd our congregations at a time marked by significant cultural chaos, spiritual confusion, and for many, disappointment and discouragement with the determined centralization wrought by the Vatican in recent years. The following profile identifies those characteristics and skills that are, from my experience, commonly found in these remarkable pastoral leaders who quietly yet bravely exercise their servant leadership in difficult times.

Where parish life is flat and uninspired, on the other hand, the characteristics and skills identified here will be largely absent.

CHARACTERISTICS

Integrity

Effective pastors and lay leaders are perceived as real people, as whole and integrated adults. They "ring true," and parishioners instinctively know they can be trusted. They possess the moral courage necessary to preach, lead, and reconcile. Their spiritual journey has taught them how to be their own person and at the same time a man or woman of the church. While they remain faithful to the gospel and to the teachings of the church, they honestly face pastoral situations that remain conflicted and thorny. Their personal and pastoral experience reinforces what Vatican II recognized: Not everything the church has taught constitutes part of its authentic tradition. Parishioners are moved when they see their pastoral ministers drawing insight and inspiration from their stories of faith and struggles with life.

The integrity of effective pastors and lay leaders requires, in the words of Catherine of Siena, that they "speak the truth in love," knowing full well that criticism will follow. The respect of their parishioners, they understand, is grounded in their commitment to be men and women of integrity.

Identity

Effective pastors and lay leaders remember that they are, before all else, disciples of Jesus Christ. Their primary identity remains grounded in their baptism. Although they may be priest, deacon, vowed religious, or lay ecclesial minister, they are first *Christians.* And because they are disciples, like other members of the faithful, they need to hear God's word, to be ministered to, and to be supported by community and friends. Grounded in their baptismal identity, they minister without hint of clericalism or spiritual superiority.

Pastors and lay ministers who make their ecclesial identity primary tend to provoke a social and spiritual isolation that is harmful to both the minister and parishioners. Their primary identity, they seem to have forgotten, is their baptismal fellowship with God's faithful.

Intimacy

No strangers to the human condition, pastoral leaders model honest, mature friendships with men and women of their own age. And with some of their friends, they have discovered soul mates—those few individuals with whom they can be appropriately intimate. (I use intimacy here in the sense of deep spiritual friendship, not as a euphemism for sexual relations.)

Without chaste, intimate friendship, the demands of pastoral leadership can be crushing. Maintaining healthy, meaningful friendships, however, can be particularly challenging for those in parish leadership roles. Does a pastor, for example, diminish his ability to minister to a family in crisis when he is a close friend to the parents? I believe he does—especially if the crisis is about the marital relationship of his friends. In spite of the challenges involved, honest, chaste intimacy with a few trusted friends remains essential for today's parish leaders. Effective pastoral ministers come to understand that emotional maturity and the support of close friendships with men and women of comparable age minimize the risk of boundary violations.

Magnanimity

It is easy to imagine the harm done by pastoral ministers who are stingy with their time, energy, and money. They simply can't reflect the magnanimity of Jesus of Nazareth or the hospitality demanded by the gospel. Effective pastoral ministers, on the other hand, have open hearts and open minds. They are gracious and welcoming and people enjoy the simple grace of their presence.

True pastoral magnanimity emerges naturally in individuals committed to prayer and contemplation. Without a true life in the spirit, gestures of magnanimity ring false. The fear and anxiety of the grasping personality betray the false words of welcome and the promises of pastoral availability.

Concern and Affection for Parishioners

Urs von Balthassar once observed that "Grace is God's affection for us." Parishioners must experience not only the ministrations of their pastor and pastoral ministers, but also they must come to experience their affection. They need to know that the parish leadership operates out of a genuine concern and care for their well-being. Tired, stretched-out pastors often don't have the psychic energy necessary to attend with care and patience to the spiritual and personal needs of their congregations. When this is the case, parishioners easily come to believe that their pastor and his associates are simply putting in their time.

Parishioners seem to know when the parish team regularly prays for them. And they seem to sense when they don't. Pastoral skills remain essential for the effective pastor and lay minister, but their regular prayer for the people they serve is the foundation of their affective concern. Sensing the genuine affection and concern of their priests and pastoral ministers, parishioners discover they are regularly praying in turn for the leadership of their parish.

An Intellectual Life

The effective pastor and lay leader, in spite of the demands placed on them, take their intellectual lives seriously. They find the time for serious reading. Their spiritual and emotional health convinces them that they must have "a life." Without serious reading, without occasional visits to the theater, the symphony, and the museum, without good novels and works of non-fiction, their imaginations begin to wither and their capacity for inspired preaching and joyful service diminishes. Moreover, their ministry is often lifeless and without creativity. And this can be deadly for a parish. I recall Mercia Eliade remarking that "spirit is strange; it has an obligation to create."

It is not surprising then to see the link between a solid intellectual life, which is always in one sense or another a life of creativity, to the pastor's spiritual life. People who attend to the needs of the mind and heart seldom find prayer a demanding or tedious experience. They bring a freshness and energy to their work as pastors and lay ministers. And they are far less likely to burn out.

Willing Rather Than Willful

Spiritual masters know that even the good should not be pursued willfully. Something happens to the human soul when an individual exercises his or her will in a willful manner rather than willingly. Healthy pastors have learned how to approach their ministry willingly. They do their best, but they force nothing. This characteristic, in itself, can be profoundly liberating. They seem to remember that the Spirit is the true shepherd of their parish. With this frame of mind, they know that doing their relative best is always good enough.

Psychologists know that willful people demand mastery and control over their personal lives as well as their environment. Willing people, on the other hand, characteristically are noted for their capacity to trust and their ability to surrender to the hidden but abiding presence of God. Effective parish leaders have mastered an important lesson—they know how to let God be God.

A Sense of Mission

The demands on the time and talents of pastoral leaders, we have seen, can be crushing. Responding to the pastoral needs of their congregations reduces the ministry of many of them to pastoral *maintenance*. The focus becomes the next funeral, the next wedding, the next visit to the hospital or nursing home, the meetings and parish events crowding his or her calendar. Working under these circumstances, the pastor or lay minister can easily lose sight of the mission inherent to the gospel—to bring the light of God's Word, the saving life and light of Jesus Christ to a world thirsting for the peace and fulfillment only the Spirit can give. "Give me a break," we hear them cry. "You want me to evangelize a confused and troubled society! I can barely make it through the week!"

Paradoxically, pastors and lay leaders who keep in mind the bigger picture, the mission inherent to the gospel, find themselves blessed with *perspective*. They know that the myriad details and demands of their pastoral work remain an integral part of the very mission of the church. This sense of mission, this graced perspective, gently reminds them of the significance of their work, and not surprisingly, it lightens their load.

A Deep and Vital Spiritual Life

Undergirding and giving form to each of the afore-mentioned characteristics of the effective pastor and lay minister is an authentic, healthy, and mature spiritual life. It is grounded in the experience of being grasped by a divine presence, a holy mystery. Touched by God's spirit, they are men and women of faith. Belief in the gospel, in revelation, in the teachings of the Church, by themselves, are not infallible signs of faith. Effective parish leaders, at least from time to time, experience the hidden power of grace erupting in their own lives and the lives of their parishioners.

Marked by these moments of grace, their parishioners come to suspect that their pastors know something about holiness. Sensing this, they come to have confidence in their priests and ministers as spiritual leaders and spiritual guides.

SKILLS

In addition to the outlined characteristics, effective pastors and lay ministers display the following skills. Ideally, these skills were developed and sharpened as part of their seminary training and ministry formation programs. In many cases, however, they were acquired "on the job" as ministers reflected on their successes and failures. A number of continuing education programs for clergy and lay ministers teach these skills, but often the priests and lay ministers most in need of them choose not to participate.

An Ability to Connect

Effective pastoral ministers, whether ordained or commissioned, are able to connect with people. As people of integrity and emotional maturity, they ring true. Parishioners and others sense they are in the presence of someone who really is interested in them, someone who respects them and takes them seriously. The priest or lay minister with this skill has enough self-confidence and poise to be present to another without the self-consciousness that blocks honest communication and relating.

Ministers who take themselves too seriously, who see themselves as a notch above the members of their congregations, seldom connect with ease. Their very style of relating is perceived as patronizing. The aloof or distant priest, deacon, or lay minister cannot help but fail when it comes to connecting with parishioners. The same is true for the isolated, lonely minister who often is both exhausted and angry.

A Capacity for Solitude

Effective pastoral leaders are not only faithful to regular times of prayer; they have learned to live *prayerful* lives. The spiritual master Brother David Stendl-Rast insists that we pray to be prayerful. A state of prayerfulness transforms our consciousness and leads to a heightened awareness. It is precisely these qualities of soul that allow busy pastors and lay leaders to move from ministerial task to task with a noticeable sense of peace of soul. Parishioners recognize this abiding spiritual calm and sense that this particular pastoral minister not only knows about God but also knows God. It is the prayerful pastoral minister who is approached for spiritual counseling and direction.

An attitude of prayerfulness almost always is the fruit of solitude. In spite of the demands placed on his or her life by the very nature of parish ministry, the effective pastoral leader has jealously guarded his or her time for quietly listening to the voice of God that can only be heard by the soul that has been stilled. In these times of contemplative prayer and quiet, the minister of the Word hears the Word that gives strength and courage, wisdom and hope. And here in prayerful solitude, the priest, deacon, religious, or lay leader understands Karl Rahner's prediction that the Christian of the 21st century will be a mystic or not at all.

A Sense of Boundaries

The mature and experienced parish leader moves easily among the various groups that comprise the congregation. Understanding that he or she is both pastoral caregiver and at the same time a member of a particular faith community, the parish leader interacts with parishioners and others as a fellow disciple of Jesus Christ—as a brother or sister—and with appropriate awareness of his or her leadership role in the community.

Effective parish leaders know who they are and understand their own human needs for friendship, intimacy, and community. They also understand the inherent danger in trying to meet these needs in their interactions with parishioners. Without question, this is one of the most difficult skills the parish leader needs to master. It can be especially challenging for those who are celibate or unmarried. More often than not, if these ministers do not have a vital, human life distinct from their ministerial roles, they stand in serious jeopardy of boundary violations.

Leadership

One of the more important signs that an individual possesses the charism of pastoral ministry is an aptitude for leadership. Until recently, many seminaries and lay ministry training programs did not rank leadership potential as a critical factor in their admissions decisions. We understand today that leadership is at the heart of parochial ministry and that effective pastors and lay ministers understand their responsibility to assume the burdens of leadership and the criticism that will inevitably follow.

Often the pastor's leadership style will be more quiet than dramatic, more subtle than direct. He and his ministry colleagues model the commitment, faith, and service they strive to evoke in the parish community. Both their presence in the local church and their pastoral care inspire and motivate. As gifted leaders, they are able to identify the various gifts of their parishioners, call upon them for the exercise of their gifts, and provide the training and support appropriate for these volunteer ministries.

An Ability to Collaborate

The "lone ranger" style of parish leadership has mostly slipped beyond the horizon. Priests now regularly work closely with deacons, pastoral associates, directors of religious education, directors of liturgy, and school principals. Together they form a pastoral team that, in reality, can be supportive and freeing as well as demanding and frustrating. In the best of circumstances, differing personalities and temperaments will make teamwork, at least from time to time, difficult. Immature, insecure members of parish teams will inevitably bring authority issues and overly sensitive egos to their ministry. Colleagues cannot help but suffer.

Still, good pastoring in today's church demands that parish leaders are healthy enough and humble enough to recognize and celebrate the ministerial gifts of their colleagues. Pastors who feel their priestly identity threatened by the church's renewed theology of ministry and the expanded pool of ministers may easily resent the successes of their colleagues and the time and energy required for healthy and creative team functioning. On the other hand, mature and secure pastors welcome the commitment and professional training, not to mention personal support, of their fellow ministers.

Doctors of Souls

Effective pastoral leaders know how to listen. They are self-possessed enough to forget about themselves, to forget about how they are doing, and to attend, as fully as possible, to the parishioner sitting in their office. I believe all good pastors and lay leaders have a certain "healing presence." Parishioners sense that just to be in their presence is a blessing. They often return to their homes after a parish organizational meeting or a visit to the rectory feeling that their souls have been expanded. They know they were taken seriously, treated respectfully, and listened to carefully.

Thomas Merton remarked that it is difficult even for saints to live together in harmony without breaking each other's "spiritual bones." Every misunderstanding, every unkind remark, every smothered resentment breaks a spiritual bone in the person offended. No matter how "small" the fracture, each broken bone carries its own spiritual pain. Pastoral ministers are meant, by the quality of their prayerful presence and pastoral training, to set these broken bones. These spiritual guides and healers are indeed doctors of souls.

Bearers of the Word

Pastoral ministers who preach well not only fulfill the most important of their responsibilities, they also sustain themselves spiritually and professionally. Rabbi Abraham Heschel once said that he preached in order to pray. It could be said that Heschel had it backwards: one prayed so that he or she might preach. Of course, good preaching flows out of a deep and mature spiritual life, but authentic preaching always leads both the preacher and congregation to experience a strong, almost urgent, need for prayer. Preaching that doesn't lead to prayer or the desire to be still in the presence of God is somehow defective.

Priests and pastoral leaders who preach well are regularly affirmed by their parishioners. And those who don't, aren't. Both as human beings and as pastoral professionals, priests and pastoral leaders need affirmation. Without recognition, appreciation, and especially affirmation, sustained ministry in today's parishes leads to psychological and spiritual exhaustion—what is commonly termed *burnout*.

CONCLUSION

Bishop Kenneth Untener was once asked why he became a priest. He responded, "It wasn't my idea!" Most pastors and pastoral ministers, I believe, are surprised to find themselves spiritual leaders in today's church. Perhaps only they can understand just how challenging and demanding their vocation is. They are not perfect. They know that. But most are committed to being as effective as possible. They deserve our support and affirmation.

Partnering

✦

REVEREND BILL GEIS, pastor
Lutheran Ministries of Southwest Oklahoma,
Lone Wolf, OK

In 1990, I became pastor of a Lutheran parish in Lone Wolf, Oklahoma, a tiny town with a population of about five hundred. This church was small, it had limited resources, and the hope and life of the town—like many in the most remote rural areas—were dwindling. Embracing the concept of partnership changed our outlook, our expectations, and ultimately, the congregation and community.

Although initial expectations were low, God blessed that ministry. By 1996 the church was a strong, growing, faith community. But it also had a reputation for taking on the tough community challenges and it earned credibility to be among the leaders of vision for the community. The congregation had become a partner with its community—with school, civic functions, other Christian efforts, a host of leaders, and every other arrangement we had opportunity to make. Partnership had become a core value for us. And we sought to expand our relationships.

We didn't do much searching before the answer came to us. It's hard to find pastors, especially to serve rural outposts. In the midst of praying about opportunities to expand our influence, three churches of our denomination (and the only ones within a 75-mile radius) experienced pastoral vacancies. So it wasn't long before I found my ministry expanded to serve three additional churches, at Granite, Elk City, and Altus. The ministry went regional overnight, through Partnership, covering six counties and 4,500 square miles in this corner of Oklahoma, where the population is about 17 people per square mile.

"Partnership" has become almost a sacred word with us. Just as Southwest Airlines capitalizes the word "Employee" in every context, so the word "Partnership" has the same distinction among our ministry Partners. Although businesses have been practicing Partnerships successfully for years, the Christian church has been largely parochial and inexperienced as an innovator of Partnerships. We are forced to play catch-up when it comes to thinking in terms of Partnerships. Our vision is limited and our structures often constraining. But we don't have to reinvent the wheel to learn and see Partnership at work. Take your kids to a fast food restaurant and they'll probably have a promotion for a feature movie in their meal pack. VISA runs ads featuring a ski lodge, and it's not until the last three seconds that you hear, "Bring your VISA card." Browse the grocery stores and look at all the cross-marketed products—potato chips with another brand's BBQ flavor, Pepsi bottles with music promotions, milk cartons with missing children's information. It's all creative Partnerships. Often, a big name will join with a much smaller player. Each benefits. Each contributes. Each builds on its distinctive recognition in the marketplace

In my denomination, we have a long history of what we call "dual parishes." By in large, this means that the pastors are shared between congregations, but the organizations do very little Partnering. While I am the only full-time pastor for the churches that form Lutheran Ministries of Southwest Oklahoma, we do not see ourselves as a dual—or in this case, a multiple—parish. We see ourselves as a fellowship of ministries sharing a common mission and vision. We share more than a pastor; we Partner through a staff, an office, and a budget. But most importantly, we Partner through our relationships and gifts, applying them beyond a single congregation to the broader picture of the body of Christ. We have a central office in Lone Wolf, and we coordinate, prioritize, resource, and operate ministry from this base. We work with the congregations and put focused time and effort into the place that needs the most ministry support. In this way, ministry—not the individual congregation's contribution of dollars or their size—dictates the priorities. For instance, in Altus, we have a very small congregation in a growing community. It requires more resources than it can give monetarily and through volunteers. We've imported volunteers from Elk City and Lone Wolf on many occasions to resource the ministry. It takes more staff involvement there, ultimately costing their other Partners through the budget.

We believe Partnership isn't just about congregations getting together. We choose to be creative about Partnership ways outside of our traditional fellowship and function. We have informal Partnerships with schools through after-school programs, safety training, science projects, music, gifted-student activities, and volunteer tutors. We share our facilities with community groups. We Partner with local government to clean up and rebuild economic and physical infrastructure. We Partner with the health department to provide an internship experience for one of our staff members' educational program. We Partner with other Christians in community action and youth activities. And most recently, we've Partnered with investors to operate a restaurant, the social hub of our small rural community, which otherwise would be closed.

The future holds incredible possibilities. We don't plan to plant any more churches; we do plan to set up ministry centers. These might include support groups, child care centers, after-school programs, seniors ministries, a youth center, parish nursing, counseling services, campus outreach, prison ministry, literacy tutors, a woman's shelter, a crisis center, and perhaps more businesses like our restaurant. To do these kinds of things would be impossible without Partnerships. We're not going to worry about who gets the credit as new Partners come together. We're going to press toward getting ministry to people in any way that works.

WHAT IT IS...WHAT IT'S NOT

Communicating the picture of Partnership, I've found it helpful to use five statements of contrast on what Partnership is...and what it is not. Actually, I always begin with the negative, because each negative anticipates a fear or problem I've found to arise in churches.

1. Partnership *is not* consolidation. Partnership *is* expanding the mission vision. Consolidation, especially in rural areas, is threatening. The Lone Wolf community has been on edge with fear of school consolidation. We fear this will mean the death of the community. Consolidation of a church is equally intimidating. And the truth is each church in our ministry is so different that consolidating would strip

each of the very identity that relates to its community. Altus is a community defined by the military. Elk City is an outpost on old U.S. 66, a stop along the road where the oil industry was once big. Lone Wolf and Granite are agricultural communities. Each congregation is positioned well for its community. I believe consolidation would serve no more than the people extremely committed their denominational roots because we would sacrifice our individual position in these unique communities. We see Partnership meeting the needs of these various communities with the resources of a broad-based team of Partners. We believe Partnership must be viewed as expansion if it's going to have kingdom impact.

2. Partnership *is not* the loss of identity. Partnership *is* the celebration and resourcefulness of diversity. When congregations begin to capture the vision for partnering, they can be so much more than they can by themselves. And they don't have to give up their individuality. We have what we call the "menu of ministries." Each church offers ministries that build on its strengths and local resources. We have people moving around in and out of the "menu" and in our view that's something to celebrate. For example we have people with musical gifts from one congregation who participate in musical productions at another church where those gifts and programs are less active. One of our churches has been successful with early childhood ministries. Another church is extremely effective with elementary school children.

And yet another church is big on family activities. Each is a part of the "menu." The more people embrace the Partnership, the more they select their volunteer time and participation in events by gifts and needs rather than location.

3. Partnership *is not* a plan to get by cheap. Partnership *is* strategic spending and risk taking. Don't sell congregations on the idea that Partnership is saving money. Tell them the real truth. It costs money, and it might actually cost more money than you are presently spending. I believe this is true for our arrangement. Overall, we spend less on pastoral services, but more on staff. We spend less on resource materials we share, but we're more aggressive about programming and launching new initiatives in ministry. Our territory has increased substantially, which has translated into higher expense allowances for transportation. We've invested heavily in communications—computers and laptops, fax machines, pagers, mobile phones, toll free numbers, web servers, and so on—all because good Partners communicate well. Communication is everything when you're Partners.

The more we get involved in ministries and in our communities, the more we want to spend. For us, that means we have to look outside the church for funding. We approached our denomination with the Partnership experiment, and they responded with substantial funding. We have Partnered with a local youth counseling agency that has a grant but lacks the personnel to administer a summer mentoring program. So we staffed the program with volunteers, and they funded advertising and program costs. We've been blessed with individuals outside of the ministry who have given gifts of $25 to $15,000 just because they witnessed some aspect of our ministry and wanted to get involved. We're in the process of buying an auto parts store that we intend to transform into a youth center and job-training program. I'm optimistic about the foundation that is evaluating our grant application toward that purchase. I'm sending our family ministry director to training in further grant writing to keep the funding agenda moving forward. Let's put it this way: Missionaries don't raise funds from the natives, they raise funds from people who believe in mission.

4. Partnership *is not* contracting for pastoral services. Partnership *is* a fellowship of ministries sharing a common vision and mission. We see our future as much bigger than having the pulpit filled on Sunday morning. We see a future where our ministry forms a canopy over the entire region. Focus on clergy is internal; focus on mission is external. One ends in death, the other in life. We believe that ministries ought to be pushing the envelope in terms of what they are doing for communities and for the Lord.

5. Partnership *is not* self-centered. Partnership *is* servant-minded. The biggest challenges Partners will face are themselves and the jealousy factor. The first question we always ask (whether voiced aloud or not) is, "What's in it for me?" But the questions I want to move you to ask with me are, "What's in it for

Christ?" "What's in it for his mission?" "What's in it for the lost?" And finally, "What gift do I have to offer this Partnership?"

HOW IT WORKS

Lutheran Ministries is organized with a lay-led board of directors. The board of directors addresses the big picture—the global issues that effect the Partnership and the interaction of its ministries. They work with me to establish the framework of policy and the broad ministry goals that the staff and I are charged to develop creatively according to our gifts and through the encouragement, training, and resourcing of lay leadership. For example, they oversee the budget of Lutheran Ministries. They coordinate scheduling of major events and functions that might affect the other Partners. They are also my accountability group. The staff, in turn, reports to me.

Each congregation has a governing assembly. That is the traditional arrangement of governance for our denomination. This assembly sends two delegates to our board of directors. It was critical for the local assemblies to delegate authority to these board members because they need to be able to make meaningful decisions for our Partnership without having each congregation approving a decision. They are also the communicators of these decisions. They have the power to hire or release anyone except the senior pastor. The pastor's calling is extended by the congregation, in this case all the congregations, which is in keeping with our denominational polity and teachings.

The board of directors are people who have really affirmed our development of people to staff our ministry. Their support enabled us to raise up a pastoral assistant, Ronald Boelte, who specializes in adult education ministries, and a director of family ministries; Mona Hunter, whose principle work is with children, youth, and parents. The board also employs a business and publications manager, Kathryn Graumann, and most recently, a volunteer coordinator, Dana Butchee. Each one of these people has been trained within the ministry and supplemented by various denominational educational tracks, seminars, and local college offerings—all while on the job.

The budget of the Partnership board of directors only deals with staff-related costs. From the beginning we chose to separate our budget into two. The Partnership would have a shared budget that would fund the cost of staff, while each local congregation would maintain a budget for its own program and facilities. The joint budget of the Partners receives its income from congregational pledges. Rather than assessing each congregation a fee to cover costs, each congregation volunteers a monthly pledge to support the shared budget. This means that financially we are not equal Partners—neither by total dollars nor on a per capita basis. We value Partnership more than "equality." That's why we operate this way. Every congregation is challenged, and each gives according to its ability. The result has been tremendous, and I believe more productive because our values are driving these commitments rather than a sense of obligation.

Each congregation's individual programs are funded by that church's local budget. We have a central printing office in Lone Wolf, so we print the worship and educational materials for all of the congregations. Local budgets pay these bills for congregational services.

Because of our centralized administration and planning, each congregation follows the same key teaching theme in Sunday worship; however, they may not have the same worship program (i.e., music, liturgy, etc.) at every church. For example, we recently did a series called, "Shaping Godly Leaders: Lessons from Titus." The teaching focus was leadership. The approach was a study of the book of Titus over the course of a month. Generally we follow themes on a monthly basis. I'm not a big fan of lengthy series. A month at a time is the kind of calendar we work with in our billing cycles, work schedules, school calendars, and so on. It just seems to work well for us as we promote what's coming up in our messages.

Because two of our churches are separated by about eighty miles, it is impossible for me to be the preacher at each of these services. Ronald Boelte, my pastoral assistant, and a lay volunteer, B. J. Armstrong, preach in the other locations. In any given location, I preach about half of the Sundays. I'm quite adamant about not publishing my whereabouts in advance because I believe worship—while it can be blessed by fine preaching—should ultimately be motivated by the Holy Spirit and a love for our Heavenly Father and His Son, rather than attraction of a particular preacher. I also want to do all I can to affirm my nonclergy leaders. I just won't stand for people picking and choosing their attendance by the preacher. On the other hand, we have an obligation to offer the highest quality we are able to give in presenting the word of God. The men I have on my preaching team are my best. And I will continue to push them to grow in their God-given abilities.

A key lesson we learned by our own mistakes is that vision needs to be constantly communicated and organizational values perpetually taught. Initially, I did a good job of rallying our congregations to become Partners. Then I rolled-up my sleeves and went to work. Two years later, I found myself saying, "Don't these people get it?" And the answer was, "No! They don't!" I had failed to keep the vision in front of them. They didn't remember my "inspirational presentation" of two years ago!

One of the changes we made was through our publications. We have two joint publications that people get every week. One is a newsletter called *Partners*. It has sections for what is going on at each various parish—not just their own. This is very important because it keeps people in touch with what is going on at the other parishes. *Partners* also leads with an inspirational article or teaching opportunity that keeps various aspects of our mission, vision, and values on the front page of ministry. We're constantly restating the vision, teaching values, creatively inspiring mission. The second publication, called *Daily Prayer,* is a devotional journey, but most importantly it is a tool for intercessory prayer. By praying together and for each other's concerns, the Partners enjoy a relationship that is strengthened by their faith and the discipline of prayer.

Both *Partners* and *Daily Prayer* are printed at our central office. Their content is generally staff-generated, but the vision is for these pieces to be a forum where the laity share their testimonies and passion about the vision of our shared ministry. Both resources are archived extensively on our web site, www.lutheranok.com. The web site has become a great tool to communicate not only within our Partnership, but also to those outside of it. The web site allows people to look in on this experiment in ministry in real time, and to review some of its past through the archives. The web site is growing daily and changing its content. It's not real slick in terms of graphics and interface. It's simple, but dynamic. It is not an occasionally updated billboard in cyberland. It's a laboratory viewing room. That's our web philosophy: Communicate, stay current, keep things in motion.

Although the congregations operate as separate entities, we get together once a month on a Sunday for an evening we call "Festive Hope," a fun, informal worship and prayer service. Here congregants can meet each other, worship together, and share testimonies about what God is doing in their churches. It's a key time for the "cross-pollination" of our people. This is where Partnership goes from the organizational model to the organic system. The Partners are real people who need to interact with each other, hear their stories, and share their prayers. They need to eat and play together. That's what organic systems do. Getting people to travel and commit time to events like this is a lot of work. But we believe it's priority work. We don't want to be a struggling institution. We want to be a living fellowship.

I've learned a lot about the organic nature of the church from the Bible. Take a close look at 1 Corinthians 12 and you'll see St. Paul tell you all about it. He says that when you're a body you need the coordination of a head. A body has individual parts, but they all serve the whole. He warns us of being jealous of others and "other systems" within the larger body. He calls us to function according to God's arrangement and distribution of gifts, rather than our impulses or mere desires. He tells us that living, breathing, feeling beings share in suffering and share in joy. He teaches us that even the weaker parts are indispensable. And he concludes, "Now you are the body of Christ, and each one of you is a part of it" (1 Cor 12:27). That's Partnership.

One Pastor, Thousands of Congregants:

NEW ROLES FOR PRIESTS AND LAY PEOPLE

✦

MONSIGNOR ARTURO BAÑUELAS, pastor
St. Pius X, El Paso, TX

Some years ago in our parish, as the numbers of priests continued to go down and the number of Catholics were going up, our parishioners were wrestling with how we were going to function with just one priest and so many parishioners.

I thought of a way to show them that a vibrant parish is about a lot more than just having a lot of priests and a lot of programs. So at a Ministry Council planning meeting, I read a letter, pretending that it was from the bishop. The letter said the following: "Because of the shortage of priests, this parish will no longer have a full-time resident pastor. He will be visiting. Given the situation, I would like for you to draw up a pastoral plan for the parish and present it to me within six months."

There was this silence, but no one left the room. I am convinced it was the Holy Spirit who inspired what followed. In a spirit of collaboration, they began to delegate and assign the different ministries, deciding which parish responsibilities each would assume. There really was little discussion; these decisions were obvious. They made a list of the community's gifts and began to call forth ministers. As leaders they felt a responsibility to tell the community about their impending future model of church, assuring parishioners that the future would be bright if all continued to stay united by working together as each person put his or her particular gift at the service of the parish and by taking greater ownership of the community. I was amazed by their lack of fear and by their courage to embrace a new approach to parish life. It was beautiful. They were taking responsibility for their parish, a role that the pastoral staff once exclusively had.

There was a sense of a new Pentecost in the council meeting. We all felt a fresh source of energy. It was evident that a new model of parish life was emerging to respond to a key moment in parish life. When all the arrangements were made, I slipped a note to a council member to ask the others: "When the priest comes, what does he do?" There was a stunning silence. Then people began to articulate the role of the priest. "We will need more spiritual direction," they said. The discussion that followed focused on their new understanding of the priest's role: No longer being the sole parish minister, main parish administer of finances and maintenance, and the one possessing all the gifts in the community. Actually, it was profoundly gratifying that the council wanted the priest to focus more on preaching, ministering to ministers, unifying the community, collaborating with ministries, doing more spiritual direction, overseeing their future growth, challenging them to work for justice, training leaders for ministry, and teaching the church's traditions. It was obvious that most had not reflected on this issue and that they needed more discussion. However, all unanimously agreed that a resident parish priest was central to the parish community. Nonetheless, their model of priest had dramatically changed, and any future resident priest would be serving a more adult Vatican II conciliar parish community.

I quickly realized that here was a vibrant community model of church that would work—if I just got out of the way. In fact, I needed to be a smaller part of the equation and the lay people of my parish a much bigger part. But the result of the exercise was the birth of a new relationship—a much more collaborative one—between priest and community. It was a new way for them to see a priest and a new way for me to see myself.

Catholic people by and large love their church and their parish. Given the opportunity and the call, an explosive dynamic happens when lay people realize that the priest does not have to be the center of this community. Christ is the center of the community. People understand that and will own up to it, if it is properly and straightforwardly presented to them. This redefined how I now could operate—mentoring, offering spiritual guidance, and sacramental care.

This exercise also forced us to ask, "Who are we?" "What is happening in our area? What are its needs?" Parishioners began to see themselves not just as a group of Catholics who happened to worship together, but as a group of people with a real mission in a specific place at a specific time. That was very powerful. They decided that to make their plan work, before they implemented any large-scale logistical changes, they needed to deepen their friendships with each other and to build an even stronger community. They became a community with a mission.

Evangelization programs and retreats flourished, and small communities developed. Ministries emerged. A new parish spirit surged, evident in parish fiestas, youth programs, increased stewardship, and outreach mission work.

As our parish leaders were wondering how exactly they should proceed with a new model of a parish that had only one priest yet thousands of parishioners and potential leaders, it quickly became obvious that more training was needed. The council approved a parish requirement that all parish ministers be trained at the diocesan Tepeyac Institute (www.elpasodiocese.org/tei) and participate in an evangelization retreat. Tepeyac Institute offers serious theological and pastoral formation programs, which run in the evenings and on weekends from September though March. During the summer it offers ongoing formation for two weeks with a variety of courses offered by a nationally recognized faculty. The courses give the ministers a theological and pastoral vision and a common language from which they can work. This has helped us tremendously to move together in the direction of forming a community with a mission that fosters the reign of God in our border reality.

In addition to this training, everyone in the parish who wants to partake in a ministry is asked to attend an evangelization retreat, which gives people an experience of Jesus and parish life in small communities. For many people this is the first time that they experience church as community, even though they have been Catholics a long time. The evangelization retreat weekend includes teachings, faith-sharing experiences, the sacrament of reconciliation, festive community meals, healing services, fellowship, hearty music, calls to conversion, missioning, and a closing liturgy with the parish community at a Sunday Mass.

Our St. Pius X parish is one of many examples of parishes inspired by the Vatican II teachings. The council tenets and a certain urgency from the priest shortage have occasioned a renewal in parish life. Parishes are witnessing a vibrancy as they affirm the rich variety of gifts with which the Holy Spirit continues to endow the Church. We have fifty-eight parish ministries that range from elderly care, parish health care, espousal abuse, AIDS ministry, Life Teen, evangelization, *Colonia* ministry, teen school mentoring, Sacred Earth ministry, Singles in Ministry, Young Adults in Ministry, to Mothers in Ministry (for young mothers), to mention a few. These include professionals as well as non-experts, but all who are well trained for their service. It became clear that the more ministries, the more present is the work of Jesus the High Priest, in whose ministry we all share.

We have learned that it is important to make a distinction between a volunteer and a minister in our parish. The term "volunteer" is not a very good or useful word because it does not respect our baptismal call. Volunteers help out in their spare time. Ministers are not "father's helpers" who assist him in their free time. Ministers participate in the priesthood of Jesus Christ, and their work has the dignity of making present Christ's own saving work. People are not baptized to be laypersons or second-class members of the church. They are baptized to be participants of the body of Christ, each according to his or her particular gift and office. Now that people are taking ownership in our parish, the recognition of gifts that people bring to the parish has become more important. We constantly recognize people's gifts in public, and people sense that their gift is their mission, their life work. Their calling has been called forth, respected, and publicly acknowledged.

Our parish budget reflects that the ministries are a priority. You may have to sacrifice certain things if you are going to spend your money training new leaders and lay ministers by enabling them to attend conferences and workshops. Each parish ministry sponsors formal expert training in their particular field of service. Theologians from leading Catholic universities and seminaries are invited to offer continuing formation, and many parishioners participate in national conferences such as the RCIA forum and the Catechetical conventions in Los Angeles. In an exciting way, the parish itself is becoming a new type of seminary for the ministerial formation of both clergy and lay ministers.

The Holy Spirit gives to the parish community the ministries it needs to fulfill its mission of fostering the reign of God in our midst. Furthermore, people are experiencing a more integrated spirituality. Putting together work life, family life, social life, and faith life by integrating them all into one vision of faith life is one of the great gifts of the church today. This is a sign of grace and of a maturing parish community and is renewing the church in our country. People see themselves as ministers, and their united witness is powerful. Additionally, while Vatican II and not the priest shortage is the cause of the emerging lay ministers,

new priestly vocations are coming from these lay leaders. So actually, the increase in lay ministers is also
adding to the increase of ordained ministers.

A ministerially collaborative model of parish that
enables and empowers the community's ministers,
that affirms the various gifts in service to the reign of
God, and that evangelizes and trains its members is
fomenting a renewal of parishes and the role of the
priests.

One Pastor, Thousands of Congregants:

CREATIVE CHAOS AND THE EVANGELISM OF CONTAGION

FATHER PATRICK BRENNAN, pastor
Holy Family Parish, Inverness, IL

My parish has close to 4,000 households, some 10,000 people. There are more than 1,500 children in religious education and 250 in high school religious education. Activities go on throughout the day and on every night of the week. We have upwards of 130 different ministries. We have a full-time counseling center on the premises. And we have but one priest, myself.

What makes my job possible in this big, sprawling, growing parish is not only a 30-person support staff—all lay people—but more than 1,000 other lay people who take ministry seriously as not only part of their church life, but part of life itself. Tom Peters, who gave birth to the excellence movement in the business world, says a good leader is "a fanatic with a vision who manages by wandering around and does his best to get as many involved in the mission as possible."

I like to see my style of pastoring in part as an attempt to do that. With the declining numbers of ordained clergy and the emergence of lay people as a much larger and multitalented group of ministers, the job of the pastor of a large church—or any church, really—is not only to encourage, but also to equip lay people for ministry. No church can survive, much less thrive, if it does not.

Under the old model of parish leadership, the trained person, usually the cleric, ministered from the top down to the target population. This was the case of the "religious professional" preparing what he thought was best for the church. In the late 1970s, I was blessed to study under Jack Shea and others in the first doctor of ministry program in the Archdiocese of Chicago. We saw in this old model the error that the clergy were assumed to be the only ones who possessed spiritual gifts. Obviously we weren't the only ones. We did a lot of doing for, and, oftentimes, doing for poorly.

The new paradigm for Holy Family Church is found in Acts 2, where the Holy Spirit brings not tranquility, but creates chaos among the people. In response, Peter boldly evangelizes about Jesus and how he can change people's lives, transforming a group of strangers into spiritual seekers. When they ask Peter, "What should we do?" he responds, "You must change your lives and be converted and baptized." The new followers of Jesus devoted themselves to communal lives. They met in the large church, but they also met in each other's homes for the breaking of bread and for prayers. They divided their goods among each other based on each other's needs. What a ministry of contagion! Day by day God added to their number people being saved. I would encourage us to look again to Acts 2 for our model of church in the future. Our churches should welcome chaos, find the Holy Spirit in chaos, and focus on evangelization and transforming folks into spiritual seekers. That spiritual seeking leads to genuine conversion, with communal life in small and large groups. The result is the evangelism of contagion that Acts 2 talks about.

The new model assumes that all of us are called to servant leadership. To do this servant leadership, we need to be trained and formed. Training and formation are not some sort of utilitarian phenomena; rather, training and formation constitute the unleashing of the gifts of the Holy Spirit. God provides the power, and in training and formation, we are enabling that power to be released and used for the common good and glory of God. As we are living in an increasingly stressful, individualized, violent, and materialistic world, we must have an even greater urgency to evangelize. Ministry flows from conversion and from baptism, as people become followers of Jesus and use their gifts for ministry in the local community.

Lay training and formation must begin in the parish. The writing of Fritz Lobinger, who has worked a lot in South Africa and parts of Europe and who has dedicated his life to the raising up of the priesthood of the faithful, has strongly influenced my views on leadership. He has said in his writings and teaching that we should do as much training and formation for ministry at the parish. We should not be sending people off to sites far away for "lay" ministry training programs because there is a message in how you do ministry training. If the ministry training is inconvenient, far away, and only a few people are sent, it conveys the message that training, formation, and empowerment are for a very few. But if you begin to house or begin to grow as much training and formation as possible at you parish, or in alliance with other parishes, it shows your congregation that the priesthood of the faithful belongs to all the baptized.

This enablement-empowerment model requires trained people at the church, and those trained persons are not necessarily clergy—they are the pastoral staff. And we are careful to point out that the pastoral staff is not to do nuevo-clericalism. The staff is not to do *for* the people; the staff does *with* the people. One of the main goals of the staff at Holy Family is to raise up ministry leaders who will then form a ministering team or community that will focus on a target population. I am constantly telling my staff that they should be working themselves out of a job, as ministry ought to become alive and existent unto itself with parishioner ownership, not overly staff dependent. Staff people ought not take the party with us when we leave the parish. We train, enable, and empower people to own the ministries and the parish.

To accomplish this, we began a ministry in our parish called "Gifted" about six years ago. It was an attempt to get away from volunteerism and help people get in touch with God's call and their giftedness and their talents. We focus on the classical gifts of the spirit that are found in 1 Cornithians 12, 13, and 14; Isaiah 11; and, 1 Peter 4:10–11, and we guide people in discovering God's call for their own lives as well as their place in the Christian community. What we are talking about here is much more than filling slots in parishes—it is helping people hear God's call. It is contemporary vocation work.

Even though we have changed formats over the years, the essence of this Gifted process is to pray; to listen to one's self; to name gifts; to seek affirmation, challenge or expansion from others; to study the needs of the parish; to listen to those needs; to name the needs; and then seek "Gift-Need Convergence." Then participants decide on the ministry and receive training and formation for it. Act, Evaluate, Learn, and Reshape are the keywords here.

The way we do Gifted is:

1. Pentecost Weekend: One time during the year we issue the call to discern gifts at each of the weekend masses.

2. Gifted—a process of gift discernment—follows, where people seek gifts of being, doing, and classical gifts of the Spirit.

3. Gifts are married to needs in eight areas of parish life: adult faith, worship, pastoral care, family faith and life, outreach and justice, youth ministry, operations (administration), and communications.

4. After gift-need convergence, training and formation are offered.

We have done Gifted in different ways throughout the year—over two nights, three nights, a single night with a lot of follow-up, on the weekend, and after Sunday Mass. Whatever the format, we are issuing a call to ministry to help folks get in touch with their giftedness. We now extend this process in weeknight workshops throughout the year. We want to splice it into our welcoming program. We splice it into the RCIA and other already existing ministries so that the entire parish is constantly considering what they have to offer and then applying those gifts to specific needs.

Gifted has been very much part of another emerging phenomenon that we call our School of Ministry, which follows Lobinger's philosophy of keeping lay training at the parish. The School has eight divisions of ministry: Adult Formation, Worship, Pastoral Care, Outreach and Justice, Operations, Youth Ministry, Communications, and Family Faith and Life, which are each asked to offer something of a formational nature, usually a series of three to four sessions for both new and experienced ministers. We publish a catalogue on all School of Ministry efforts every six months. The School of Ministry also oversees "Called," a two-year lay ministry training program. The folks meet most Thursday evenings from fall to spring, and some Saturdays. This results in a certificate in pastoral leadership.

Along with this training, it is very important to us at Holy Family to do liturgical commissioning for these emerging ministries. Throughout the year, we commission catechists, liturgical ministers, Small Christian Community leaders, neighborhood ministers, and others.

When we found some of our people hungering for more than just the two-year leadership program, we invited the Loyola–New Orleans Certificate of Advanced Studies Program to our school, which now offers a Certificate of Specialized Studies. Participants attend a series of six weekend sessions over two years, resulting in a Specialized Certificate in Parish Life and Administration.

A group of women came to me saying that they had not finished their bachelor's degree and were thinking of a second career in ministry. We brought in Dominican University's B.A. courses on ministry.

These sessions are held on Wednesday afternoons and evenings. Some other folks wanted this at the master's level, so we invited in Catholic Theological Union. CTU courses are offered via interactive TV from the south side of Chicago to our parish in Inverness, about fifty miles away. Interaction with the instructor and other students in the city is immediate. We most recently have added Essential Catholicism and the Catholic Scripture School to round out our School of Ministry offerings.

There is a corollary that is very interesting when people realize they are dealing with a call to utilize the gifts of the Holy Spirit. They begin to see their lives as a holistic stewardship of time, gifts of the Holy Spirit, and material resources. Since we have been moving in this direction of stewardship and vocation, we have seen our collection go up considerably, as well as the number of people who seem to be hearing the call from God to be involved in the body of Christ. So, not only do more people want to contribute their gifts and resources, more people want to be a part of a church that needs and employs their unique contributions.

The lateral, empowerment model of ministry has made me a teacher-pastor. Many of us on staff resource the various modules and series that are part of our School of Ministry. As staff, we are always challenged to stay fresh and to read that we might resource/train others. Our staff is always doing both direct delivery of services within our competencies and empowerment and training of parishioners. It truly is an exciting, collaborative model. The leaders of all 130 ministries meet with staff on the second Tuesday of the month at 7 P.M. for faith sharing, more training, and formation and business. This meeting has greatly improved co-laboring and communication, helping us to avoid silo-ing the various ministries.

✦

As a Church Changes:

A PROTESTANT PERSPECTIVE

✦

REVEREND MARK BECKWITH, rector
All Saints Episcopal Church, Worcester, MA

I serve in an Episcopal parish that was founded in 1835. It is a large, imposing, Gothic church, a glorious building. People were proud of its heritage and of the building itself. We also have the oldest men and boys choir in the country. This is both a gift and a curse at the same time. We have all these boys, one of whom is my son, wearing ruffled collars and singing like angels. Many people want this tradition to continue until the Messiah comes again, an expectation that much of the church has carried with it for a long time. We have had many generous ancestors who have left us with endowments, part of which pays for all the needs of the organ. People come from all over the country to play it. It is a fabulous icon.

But, on the other hand, if you are in a congregation this old, it is like rock—unmovable. Among my predecessors, six former rectors have become bishops. All Saints is one of those classic, downtown Episcopal churches that suggests power and prestige, and its reputation in the community is that of well-connected church. The subtext is that if you go there you will meet the right people and it will serve you well in the larger community. Yet, at the same time, throughout its history All Saints has been a multiracial congregation. The member who has the deepest roots in the congregation—going back six generations—is an African-American woman. In Worcester, if your family goes back three or four generations in the city itself, it is often the case that you are either African American or Nipmuc Indian. And so, although we are considered to be a pretty tiny place, we have a socioeconomic swing that is very wide. We have CEOs and doctors as well as people who are one paycheck from being on welfare.

I was called to be rector of All Saints in 1993. I was told that the congregation wanted to change. It clearly needed to change because, as a downtown church in a neighborhood that was becoming more marginalized economically, it could no longer exist as an upper-middle-class ecclesiastical bastion. The church said it wanted to change, but was unsure how to go about it. When I came I did not meet with any resistance, but I found entropy everywhere. People had a deep faith and a desire to change and grow, but they had no models for doing so. They had no idea of how to become this part of the body of Christ that both embraces the reality of life around the church as well as the history and tradition embedded there. That is the heritage of the congregation—some of it is Yankee stuff, some of it is Episcopalian, and some of it is unique to Worcester.

And then there was me. I came from a smaller urban church in New Jersey. I had experience working in congregations and getting people organized and excited about pursuing a common mission. I came with the hubris of having developed homeless and AIDS ministries, both of which I assumed could be replicated in Worcester.

I am mindful of the tension between being willful and being willing. For the first two years at All Saints, I was the most willful new rector that the church had ever seen. I was determined that through my will I would move this congregation in the direction that they wanted to go and the direction that I wanted to go. The church that I served in New Jersey was much smaller. I compare it to being captain on a small attack boat. We could move quickly and make changes without too much difficulty. When I came to All Saints, I felt that I was on the deck of a fully loaded oil tanker, and I was not sure that I was its captain. There were several people who were claiming the captain role, mostly by default—carrying out tasks that had long been neglected. I read once that a fully loaded oil tanker requires 14 miles of open ocean to negotiate a 90-degree turn. I kept reminding myself of this little factoid. Change does not happen easily. Churches are slow to change. We need a lot of room and a lot of time to navigate. And I needed to change from being a willful and ego-driven rector to a God-centered and willing servant.

On the other hand, the area surrounding All Saints was changing a lot faster. Lots of storefront churches sprang up and disappeared, and businesses came and went. We are the oldest institution in the neighborhood, a fact that has brought considerable benefit to the neighborhood because people could look at the building and sense stability in the midst of an unstable neighborhood. This tension between stability and instability is not something we want to avoid.

The reality of our neighborhood helps develop our ministry, and we bring that neighborhood reality into our church in a variety of different ways to agitate how we might become something new. At the same time, as we come out of our grand space and into this marginalized community, we offer something as well—it is mix and match. We both bless and are blessed by our neighborhood.

I often say that our congregation is akin to a temple, as opposed to a synagogue. In the Jewish tradition, the temple is built at the center; it is the citadel where people gather. We need to honor the temple model because it is part of our history. It is indeed a beautiful temple, and a lot of very citadel-like things happen in the context of temple. At the same time we need to develop the synagogue model of our religious community. A synagogue is much smaller and can shift more quickly. A synagogue is more on the order of a cell group that identifies a mission, acts that mission out, lets it go, and celebrates it so that the community can move on to another. We have been trying to live with both, to live in this tension between temple and synagogue, between Old New England money and Yankee ways and values and newer, contemporary, less affluent people who are much less versed in what being a "parishioner" is, and actually not caring as much about membership as they are about having their needs met and their souls fed.

Episcopalians are known for lot things. One is for being the "frozen chosen." Another is for living in tension between being Protestant and Catholic. In this congregation, we live in between what was and what is coming, between tradition and contemporary, and between Yankee and multicultural.

I can think of two recent examples of life in our congregation that highlight how we are changing. The first is the antiracism training that about forty of us in the congregation went though. The National Episcopal

Church has put together an exquisite antiracism training program. When we presented the program to the congregation, we went though a long process to introduce it and identify why we thought this was necessary. Many people think our congregation is wonderful because we are so diverse. Maybe 20 percent of the congregation is of minority background, which, in my mind, doesn't threaten anyone who is in the majority. People can feel really good about having minority people in the congregation, but 20 percent or so is neither large enough nor vocal enough to really have an impact on the overall direction of the congregation. Prejudice gets acted out in unconscious ways all the time. We decided that we needed to look at prejudice and to see how it operates. There are several people in our parish who have been though the causes of the last thirty years and said: "I have done that. I know all about prejudice. I know all about racism. I am beyond that." Those are precisely the folks that we needed to bring in to the process.

As we went though this antiracism training, we discovered that it is an ongoing process. Everybody has some pain around it either as a perpetrator or as a victim. Everyone needs to talk about that pain in a safe environment and tell his or her stories.

Perpetrators have a lot of shame about their participation as racists and victims have anger, if not bitterness. As we tell these stories, we become more enlightened to the reality of each other's lives and we build a stronger community. Racism is a sinful disease that has affected and continues to affect everyone.

The second thing that we have learned to do to embrace change is to see ourselves as the gathered community of imperfect folk at different stages of life and of spirituality and of different backgrounds. We make it clear that whoever comes to church on Sunday is welcome to receive the gifts of the table. At the presentation of the Eucharist, I say, "All who seek God and are drawn to Christ are welcome to receive the Lord's Supper." Technically I am not supposed to say this. In the Episcopal Church only the baptized are welcomed to receive the Eucharist. I do not draw the distinction between the baptized and unbaptized. We have people who come from non-Christian backgrounds or, which is often the case, no religious background. It may have required a significant emotional effort to come through the doors in the first place. My feeling is that if we put up other barriers to say we welcome you here but you can not participate in this feast that everyone else can have because you are not old enough or you have not had water sprinkled over your head or you have not been immersed in the pool of new life, some folks will not come back again. People have a lot of experience being excluded, and many do not know what it means to be included. So what we do is invite anyone who would like to come to take communion.

Many people in the congregation tell me that this open invitation to the Eucharist is one of the most important things that we do. It is surprising the people who tell me how important this is to them because it seems to bridge the tension between old and new. They see the benefit of opening to door and table to anyone who wants to receive. We offer communion with the expectation that anyone who comes will then be baptized. In fact, this has often been the case.

We live in the tension between this heritage and what is unfolding. Does it work? Sometimes it does not work at all, and we have to give something up and try it in a different way. What is clear to all of us who are in leadership at All Saints is that we need to keep at it. We need to continue to honor our roots and also offer other expressions as well. We need to appreciate the patience that is required to continue this change, to honor the fact that no one really knows how to do it correctly. I think all of this is a local issue and needs to be figured out on a local level. You have to figure out your own tension, how you are going to address it, how you are going to honor both sides of it, and how you are willing to be open to the Spirit that allows something new to emerge. If *we* only allow it. I'm still trying to learn that.

As a Church Changes:

A CATHOLIC PERSPECTIVE

FATHER WALTER CUENIN, pastor
Our Lady of Help of Christians, Newton, MA

W hen I got to Our Lady Help of Christians about eight years ago, it was a tired parish, physically, emotionally, and spiritually. We have 2,600 families and a huge plant, occupying about four city blocks in Newton, Massachusetts, a suburb of Boston. We have a high school, various other buildings, and two convents. The church, a once-grand edifice, was dingy and dark. When I arrived there was one nun, two priests, and little inspiration about the place. There had even been talk of closing the parish down. Obviously things had to change. I wanted to help put life back in to what had been the mother church of our city.

Today, we have a completely renovated church and the two old convents are now shelters, one for victims of domestic violence, the other for women who have just completed drug rehab so they are able to live with their families for awhile. The school and all our programs are run by lay people, and the sister serves as a pastoral associate. I am the only priest; the two priest associates who were there when I arrived went on to other assignments after a year.

We are not a parish that continues to wail about the shortage of priests. Instead we are a parish that acknowledges that the largest religious group in the America is nonpracticing Catholics. And we set out to do something about it, to create excitement and involvement, and to be a parish where you have no choice but to be involved. We still have a long way to go, but we concentrated on three things—good staff with a common vision, hospitality, and the restoration and then the use of a beautiful worship space.

The first thing I did was to invite Sister Marie LaBolita to come on as a pastoral associate. I hired a laywoman, Mary Ellen Cocks, as a second pastoral associate. We priests need to have women on staff in key positions; we need the feminine dimension. I tried to send a signal. As a leader, you need to send some clear signals about a direction, even as you are sensitive and listening to what is being said. You cannot sit back and think, "Well, maybe today I'll be inspired."

Early on we had a Town Meeting for the entire parish so everyone could be heard. We brought in facilitators to help people in small groups figure out what they wanted to do. We found that people loved this church, and given the opportunity, they would do anything to not only have it survive, but to thrive.

One big thing that I tried to instill immediately when I got to Our Lady's was to develop a sense of hospitality. Roman Catholic parishes tend to be like fortresses, where just to get a child baptized you have to scale the Berlin Wall. I thought that the real model should be an attitude that said, "We are here for you and we open our arms and welcome everybody." That being said, then we can work out the details.

For example, when I first got to Our Lady's, there was a strict policy on how weddings were scheduled. It was impossible to even find out if the church was available for a specific date, let alone book it. Now when people call and say they want to be married in our church, we don't put them through the third degree. Our staff is instructed that when a couple calls, to say, "Congratulations; this must be a wonderful time for you," or something like that. There is time enough to talk about dates and flowers and caterers and the more serious issues of preparing for a church marriage.

We constantly try to look at everything we do and ask, "How can we open up the place? How can we reach those nonpracticing Catholics? How can we reach into the neighborhood of which we are part?"

One of the things I have always done at Christmas and Easter midnight masses is to say: "It's so good to see you tonight. We are a spiritual community that welcomes everyone. We welcome the divorced and the married, the single parents, twice married, devout Catholics, Catholics who are holding on by their fingernails, gays, and straights."

You start doing this when the large crowds come, and the word travels. People know this to be a place where they can come even if their lives do not fit every detail of the "ideal" Catholic model.

We have a lot of Jewish people in Newton, and one of the synagogues is right down the street from the church. A few years ago it was vandalized during the night, and swastikas were painted on the building. It was a terrible thing. We had to do something to respond. These are our neighbors, so we decided that at Sunday morning Mass we would have a walking homily. We walked down the street to the synagogue, and we prayed together that this would never happen again. We try putting into practice what we have been preaching.

The other priority was the restoration of the church. It became a vehicle for people to make a deeper commitment to the community. We needed to raise millions of dollars to restore the church to its former glory, and when people began to understand it was their church and it would be a beautiful place they would worship in, where baptisms and weddings and funeral and public events would occur, they came on board.

But just to have a beautiful building wasn't enough. It was what was happening inside that was far more important. One of the things that we wanted was to move the choir from the loft in the back to the front of the church. This was not easy, and we worked on it slowly, inexorably, for several years. Now they are down front and it is wonderful. You can see the kids— we can shake hands—we can be interactive. But there is always pain with change. Some choir members left the church. This happens—it is something we all face in ministry. No matter how carefully you proceed, no matter how much time you spend in process, not everyone can go in the direction that you are moving. This is okay; perhaps there are other places where they will be more comfortable. You must be prepared for some people to tell you that the idea you like the most is the absolute worst idea imaginable.

We also put in a full immersion pool for baptism. In the Boston area, there are not many churches that have full immersion pools. Again, we spent years working up to this. For a transition, we used a big decorated salad bowl for immersing babies. This was to get ready so that people would think about immersion, and when we got to the restoration, we could put in the full pool and it wouldn't be so drastic a change. So now, baptism is wonderful, water splashing everywhere, and it has taken on a whole new place in the Catholic experience. It is central now. Through baptism, we see that everybody is part of ministry.

These changes, although not easy, helped us to grow as a church community. We spent about four years on the process with committees and studying. We went to other churches, to public meetings. We took time. While I am basically an impatient man, you must take time to allow things to percolate, develop, for people to own the idea. It may be your vision, but if it is not theirs as well it is doomed to failure. I do not think we could have raised the funds if we didn't have a large base of support. It's wonderful now to enjoy it. But going though the changeover, I had some days when the pain of change just about did me in.

As part of the change in contemporary Catholic life—as was witnessed in the "old" Our Lady's turning into the Our Lady's of today—we have nurtured and brought forth lay ministry. Because we are a big Catholic parish, we have a lot of sacramental life in this church. We have about 200 baptisms, 150 funerals, and 100 weddings annually. It is an enormous process. Since I am the only priest, I have to be involved in some parts of that. But many times I do not, and I have turned over huge portions of this to lay people. We have a bereavement ministry, which goes to the homes and plans the funeral and the funeral liturgy. The pastoral associates go to the funeral home and do the wake service, they then go also to the cemetery. It gives them, especially the women, real pastoral prayer leadership.

At first, this took a while to put into effect. Some said: "Why not a priest? His prayer is more important that a woman's prayer." But we worked it through and stuck with it. It has proven to be a wonderful thing. Not only did it save my sanity, the enrichment that the pastoral associates bring to the entire funeral experience is wonderful.

It is a major change in the way Catholic parishes, especially in the Northeast, were used to operating. Not simple. You have to work it out, talk about it, and explain it. Then you have to be willing to do it and follow though with it over a period of time to really make it happen.

But, again, I realize not everyone will like everything you do. I think it was first ingrained in the seminary and then confirmed in my thirty years as a priest: to always have people like you, as if this were the litmus test of your worth. I have learned though being a pastor and going through an extended period of radical change that it is okay to have differences of opinion and to realize that not everyone will appreciate what you are doing. When we started our gay and lesbian faith-sharing group, not everyone in the parish was happy to see it published in the church bulletin. One family left the parish. They told me they were tired of going to Easter Mass and coming home and explaining to their kids why we have to welcome gays into our church. These are complicated questions, and they do generate tension. On the other hand, real leadership and the ability to change communities is not just to change the outside or inside of the buildings. It is about changing the heart and a whole mentality of what a parish community truly is—changes that involve a lot of pain and a lot of happiness, too.

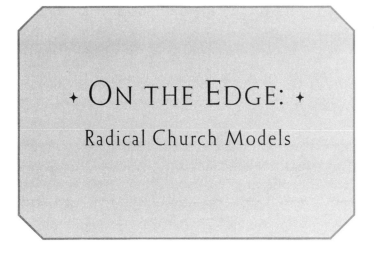

⋆ ON THE EDGE: ⋆
Radical Church Models

Church Planting:

FINDING ISLANDS OF HOPE

REVEREND DUANE ARLEDGE, minister of missions
Riverside Baptist Church, Denver, CO

R iverside Baptist Church is located right in the heart of Denver. We are just a few blocks from Mile High Stadium, and around us are the conflicting interests of a poor neighborhood—of recent Hispanic immigrants and groups trying to gentrify this old, dilapidated neighborhood. The people who come to Riverside generally do not live in the surrounding neighborhood; they come from all parts of the city.

As with many churches in similar demographic quandaries, we struggled with how to "reach our community for Christ." And even though we have created working ministries that provide for our neighbors' basic needs such as food and clothing, we believe that God has caused us to rethink how we reach people; to think *kingdom* growth, not *church* growth. What a lot of pastors mean, and what I always meant in previous church experience when I said let's "reach our community for Christ," was really that I wanted to fill up our building. In our pastoral meetings at Riverside, we find God tearing down that ingrained idea. The great commission is focused on "go." There is nothing in the great commission about our glory. It is all about His glory. The kingdom of God should grow, even if numbers increase in the church down the street and not yours.

We have also learned to replace the concept of *megachurch* with *metachurch*. *Meta* means change, so instead of building huge megachurches with thousands of members and hundreds of programs, we are talking about churches making some major shifts in their thinking. One of those shifts would be pastors changing their minds about the way they do church. They would no longer think of church as a building but a "body." When pastors are free from the denominational model and begin to change their mind about structure and strategy to reach people, they are open to new ideas of building God's kingdom, even if that kingdom is not inside the four walls of their church building. A metachurch refuses to limit the size of its ministry to a single campus, building, identity, or location.

So we decided instead to build a strong central hub church and place spokes all over the metro area. These "spokes," or church plants, would touch the people who Riverside, because of its limiting demographics and location, never could. We have really adopted a vision, which we believe is from God, that we were called to be a hub and plant churches all over the city. As of now, we have more than twenty-five vital congregations that we have planted, including a biker congregation, a truck stop church, and Vietnamese, Japanese, and Indonesian fellowships.

After planting dozens of churches, and seeing some that didn't make it, we have learned that the person who pastors the new church is absolutely vital to its success. As a result, the initial stage of our church plant process begins with qualifying the candidate for pastor. We believe everything rises and falls on leadership. I'd rather not start something than start something with a bad leader. So although there are a lot of places in and around Denver that are in desperate need of a church, we're waiting on God to provide the right guy for the right place.

When we assess candidates, we look for thirteen characteristics that are based on research from a year-long study of successful church planters. We're looking for lifelong patterns where they've exhibited these characteristics rather than hearing their philosophies on church planting. These men should have faith to attempt great things and overcome obstacles. They should be flexible, their spouse should cooperate in the initiative, and they should be able to galvanize people around them and communicate a vision. We don't ask candidates, "What would you do if," but "What did you do when." I'm looking for spiritual qualities and characteristics, people skills, and winsomeness. There are a lot of people in ministry who are effective in what they're doing, but they are not wired for church planting.

Although this interview and assessment of the candidate's qualities is not absolutely inerrant, it does give us indicators of his potential. If the person seems to be a likely candidate, my next step is to pray. I ask God if we should partner with this person.

Once we believe that God is leading us to partner with this church planter, the next step is seeing where the candidate wants to plant a church, then looking for his fit with a target community. Some people come to us and say, "God's moving me to the west," so we just explore the city and drive through the neighborhoods. We had one young guy recently come here from seminary, and when we showed him areas that could use a church, in one neighborhood he and his wife saw a lot of young moms and young professionals. They simultaneously began to have an overpowering feeling that God wanted them to work with these people.

Once we've found a fit between the person and the place, Riverside begins its partnership with the new church. We do help them financially, but only for two to three years. John Maxwell says that a real leader can raise money, men, and morale. We hold to that—if a pastor believes in his mission and calling strong enough, then we believe he can raise the money necessary to keep the church going.

The pastor becomes a staff member of Riverside, but we intentionally do not underwrite all of his funding. All of his funds flow into Riverside, where they get benefits such as our annual audit and our accounting staff. They become a legal entity through their affiliation with us, and they do not have to pay fees for bookkeeping, checking, or banking. Essentially, we're holding their hands while they're young.

My role in this is as these pastors' supervisor, coach, and mentor. I'm more available to them than to anyone except my family. I work with them to set mileposts, such as the number of core group members they need to launch their first public meeting. These mileposts drive their work rather than the calendar. All of the pastors attend a basic training course for church planters, which is a program our state mission board purchased rights to and rewrote to fit the context of Colorado. Riverside pays for the pastor to attend—it's our investment in them. We encourage the pastor to also bring a few of his core members to help him think through the church's strategy at the workshop.

Our goal is for the church to be autonomous and self-governing, but we ask each pastor to remain in a family-like relationship with Riverside. We host a monthly meeting for all of the pastors in our church plant network, and right now we invite twenty-five to thirty pastors each month, some of whom have been pastors of self-sustaining churches for more than five years. It's at this meeting where these pastors can network, rub shoulders with guys of like nature. This meeting is not your typical denominational pastors meeting. We really try to cultivate an atmosphere of complete openness where any pastor can be completely transparent—they can reveal their true struggles without fear of criticism.

Here are some of the things we have learned from our church plant program:

✦ Terminology does matter. Our planted churches have their own name and identity—we do not call them a mission church—we refer to them as a church from the very beginning. We want them to feel like a "real" church.

✦ We expect our planted churches to reproduce Riverside Baptist's theology and philosophy for ministry—not its methodology.

✦ We need satellite churches to reach beyond geographical, cultural, language, and economic barriers.

✦ We will never accomplish the great commission if we wait for our seminaries.

+ There are two irreducible minimums for starting an effective church: a visionary leader and a viable location.

+ We believe with every fiber of our being that we need a renewed interest in strong, relevant, biblical preaching.

+ It is usually easier and more efficient to start a new church than revive or retool an old stagnant church.

+ Usually we will get more resistance from territorial pastors around us or leaders of denominations when starting new churches than we do from anyone else.

The city of Denver needs dozens and dozens of churches. To make that happen, our church planters must sponsor other church planters. If I help a guy plant a church and he never intends to plant another one, I think that's hypocritical. We've decided that we're not interested in investing in people are who aren't interested in carrying it on. And we're pursuing this in other areas as well, such as encouraging bivocational or volunteer pastors, like the man who pastors our Indonesian congregation and owns an architect business as well. We are praying for people to infiltrate communities and shepherd twenty-five to thirty people, maybe in the style of a house church. We want to see small Christian communities in mobile home communities and multifamily dwellings, where we're statistically not seeing a lot of people coming to church right now.

In all this, Riverside is the catalyst and the hub. But the work doesn't begin and end here—as our church plants continue to contextualize the Gospel for the Denver area's varied communities, we hope to reach people through a movement that replicates itself and infiltrates the many niches of this complex city.

Reaching Bikers:

CHURCH IN THE WIND

REVEREND GARY DAVIS, pastor
Church in the Wind, Denver, CO

I am not your typical pastor. I ride a Harley, have long hair and a beard, and wear leather when I preach. My church, the Church in the Wind of Denver, is more than five years old and services more than 150 families in the community; many of them from the biker lifestyle. Forty percent of the congregation are bikers, and 60 percent are people who just don't fit in traditional churches.

I became a Christian in August 1973 while my riding group went to Sturgis Bike Week in South Dakota. When my friends came home, I told them about this Jesus I had met, and within three months, I was out of the group. I wandered to and fro looking for a church that would accept me and my chosen style of transportation, but I found mostly unacceptance in traditional churches. I wanted to fit in, so eventually I changed to be what they expected and wore a suit and rode a Honda Goldwing, but I was miserable not being who I really was. So I gave up on God's people, but not on God. I studied the Bible independently, hoping to find answers.

At a biker swap meet one day I realized that there were a lot of people there who needed to know about Jesus Christ, but I knew they would run into the same problem I had, unacceptance, because of they way they looked. I prayed for God to send someone to witness to them about the love of God, now knowing that He would send me. I began to witness and bring them back to church with me, but the church I was going to did not know what to do with these strange people who did not look or act like them. Many of the church leaders made sure I knew I was not qualified to be a pastor, or a missionary, so I kept praying for God to send someone else to teach these people who were not getting saved.

But I discovered that if the call of God is on your life, you will not be happy until you do what God has called you to do, regardless of what people tell you, so I began to teach Bible studies in my home. Sometimes we studied until 2:00 A.M. because so many had questions and they needed answers. My wife, Diana, developed a food bank in our garage and gathered durable goods to meet the practical needs of this community. We held potlucks and fellowships to encourage whoever was interested. Diana taught women's studies. And so we served God, using 30-plus percent of our income to finance everything ourselves.

Then, in 1994, while my wife and I were on the way home from Sturgis Bike Week, we reevaluated our ministry. We were physically tired, emotionally wounded by a close couple we had trusted, spiritually drained, and financially broke. We decided to quit the ministry and take a year off to heal. At that same time, Riverside Baptist Church was putting together an outreach called "Arms Around Denver" and was looking for ministries like ours, small, effective, but without support, to wrap the love of God around the city of Denver. Reluctantly we interviewed with Duane Arledge, the director of missions, and by the grace of God we were invited to be a part of that operation. We were energized again, but this time we received training, resources, prayer support, encouragement, financial support, accountability, and acceptance. We were built up in the body of Christ and encouraged to finish the call God had placed on our lives to "reach the lost and teach the found" in a special group that no one else wanted because they were "church-damaged" goods. (Most were rejected in traditional churches, many were taught false doctrine that trapped them in bondage, and many were prodigal sons and daughters looking for a way back to God.)

We used an old church building, which the Denver Association of Southern Baptists gave us for $1 a year, and Riverside Baptist paid all the utilities for a couple of years for Bible studies and potlucks, but it wasn't working. The neighborhood didn't welcome these "bikers" and thought we were a bike club. They already had gangs to deal with—they did not want us too. Finally God gave me a vision to have regular church services on Friday nights. Clubs give people a chance to go and ride, but what they really need is a place to learn and serve. So I went back to Riverside for help, and they gave us free use of their wedding chapel. They helped us plan and finance a biker Sunday in October using their parking lot. More than 150 people came. They heard an encouraging message, ate a free lunch, played biker games, and we promoted the idea of church. We began the church November 1, 1996, and fifty-six people attended the service.

We enlarged the food bank, gathered a core group, I became a licensed pastor, and we went to church planting "boot camp" and began the process of making a safe place to worship the Lord. Riverside allows us to reach this group of people and teach them without using traditional methods. We teach that God wants a relationship with his people, not religious acts. God is interested in what is in our hearts, not the clothes on our backs. God has a plan for each of his children; life is not just a matter of luck of random experiences. We have an acronym for the Bible: **B**asic **I**nstructions **B**efore **L**eaving **E**arth, our owner's manual and operating instructions. We meet on Friday evenings for services, which keeps people out of the bars and allows us to attend secular biker functions on the weekends to witness to others. We do weddings, funerals, baby dedications, and baptisms just like other churches, but we adapt our methods without compromising the message that Jesus Christ is Lord and Savior.

In February 2000, Riverside Baptist helped us move from being a mission church to being a sister church standing on our own resources. By the grace of God, there are seven "Church in the Wind" churches operating nationwide. Four are Southern Baptist (Lindale and Longview, Texas; Denver, Colorado; and Farmington, New Mexico), one is Rhema Fellowship (Midland, Texas); one is Christian International (Las Vegas); and one is Independent Baptist (Kansas City, Kansas), but all are proclaiming Jesus Christ as Lord. We are trademarked and have established criteria for starting Church in the Wind sister churches. We have joined together as a national church-planting fellowship of churches to pray for each other and teach biblical truth. Denomination is unimportant as long as basic truths are the foundation of teaching and unification of the body of Christ is practiced.

We have web sites for several of the churches so people who are traveling can visit a church that will accept them away from home. Visit www.churchinthewind.org to explore our site.

Our vision is to have a Church in the Wind in every city of every country where there are bikers who need Christ. We hope to establish a thrift store here in Denver to help finance the building of more churches as well as meet the needs of the local community, and to start a training center for disadvantaged people. We will travel wherever necessary to help another church or group reach out to this special group to spread the news of a risen Savior.

Seeker-Sensitive Catholic Parishes

FATHER PATRICK BRENNAN, pastor
Holy Family Parish, Inverness, IL

An honest look at the Catholic Church shows that it essentially is not connected to the very people it is supposed to serve—or has the potential to serve. Studies on Catholic parishes by the Movement for a Better World suggests that we are missing 75 percent of our potential, or the 75 percent of Roman Catholics who are functionally unchurched. They do not know Catholic teachings; they do not know about Vatican II; they do not know the rich storehouse of spiritual tradition that is ours. They do now know how the Catholic faith can be a template for a happy and holy life.

A lot of that has to do with the way the church is structured. And, as congregations shrink, get older, and watch resources for ministry evaporate, they are forced to choose between remaining a Maintenance Church, staying with the tried and true programs, or becoming a dynamic Mission Church that finds new ways to reach not only its people, but also to connect with younger people and people of different racial and ethnic backgrounds.

The broad term for these "unreached" and "unchurched" people is "Seekers," and it can include anyone—from the Catholic who's attended Mass for years to the young, single professional who has never set foot in a church. Folks in the Baby Boom generation as well as Generation X and adolescents are called "Seekers" in the evangelical world. For a church to stay vital, it must target these people. And the research suggests that if you embrace this mission style of being of being a church, your numbers will increase, the resources will be there for ministry, and the congregation will maintain a younger edge as well as being connected to other age groups.

The Catholic Church is loaded with one type of potential seekers—people for whom the water of Baptism has been poured, but who have not had a genuine experience of evangelism or conversion. There are also the nonbaptized and baptized Protestants who may feel a calling to the Catholic Church. The Rite of Christian Initiation of Adults revealed these groups to us years ago.

What are Seekers after? They are looking for meaning. Many are reaching a point in their careers and lives that, despite their personal success, they are looking for meaning and belonging. Many are looking for a shared spirituality for their family. Others are searching for an inner healing that only spirituality or that spirituality in combination with other forces can bring. They are looking for good worship and good preaching that offers a spirituality that is vibrant. They are looking for welcoming congregations rather than a group of isolated individualists. They are looking for ministries that help them live.

Seekers are people who are awakening to their need for spirituality, which is more important to them than institutionalized religion. They tend to be eclectic, having built their spirituality from a variety of sources in the secular world, such as psychology. They also build spirituality from religious traditions, borrowing from many different denominations and religions. If they come from a religious tradition, they are not necessarily tied to it.

Tom Beaudoin, in his book *Virtual Faith: The Irreverent Spiritual Quest of Generation X* (Jossey-Bass), describes people in their 20s as formed by popular culture. If we think we can minister by diminishing the pull of popular culture, we are being naïve. They want to experience their God and spirituality in ways that are congruent with that popular culture.

Tom Beaudoin's banner line to churches run by folks older than he, older than his generation, is: "Stop feeding us bad religion. We are hungry for spirituality." People in their 20s are attracted to mysticism, but they are also irreverent. They are suspicious of institutions, but they are experiencing an attraction and a return to Jesus. Personal experience is very important to them. They want to experience God. When they come to church, they want worship to be an experience. That's why at Holy Family—utilizing both the richness of our Catholic tradition and call of the popular culture, and building on some of the innovative approaches Willow Creek has pioneered—we put an emphasis on good singing, good music, preaching, and drama.

Generation Xers want belonging and community so much that many seek it via the Internet. They are people who know the suffering of broken relationships that they grew up with. They are wresting with ambiguity, and for some this leads to forms of fundamentalism for security and direction. Yet many can embrace and wrestle with the ambiguity that is involved with being a faithful person.

In the recent study *Young Adult Catholics: Religion in the Culture of Choice* (University of Notre Dame Press), Dean Hoge concluded that many Catholics are not going to be swept along by guilt and obligation any longer. "These are spiritual people awaking to their spiritual needs, and they will go where they are fed," Hoge states. "They are aware of choice when it comes to parish or church. Gen X folks, especially Catholics, are spiritually illiterate of their tradition. Yet they are somehow attracted to Catholic identity, but because they have not been yet given any skills in Catholic apologetics or apologetics of any sort, they are bowled over by other more passionate young adults who are part of other evangelical denominations."

Jeremy Langford wrote in *Church Magazine:* "Catholic church: wake up and seek the Seekers. Go to where they are. Don't expect them to come to us." That's the genius of the evangelical movement—they go to where Seekers are. Go to coffee shops, go to bookstores, go to where young adults hang out. Langford states that this age group is a culture that is sensitized to issues of justice, charity, and compassion. Perhaps we can hook young adults in the experience of small groups, small Christian communities, and justice and compassion work. Perhaps the worship will come later, if we can attract them with these things that they seem naturally attracted to.

To reach Generation X, we at Holy Family created two new, intentional ministries. One is called Journeys, which has a 30s tinge to it, reaching more of the older young adult population. People in their 30s gather in small Christian communities and book discussion groups, worship together at a young adult Mass, and minister to high school teens in their small group. They gather young adults on a Thursday night just for refreshments, conversation, and prayer.

Our other program, interestingly, was founded after a Catholic went to Willow Creek and decided that he was called back to the Catholic Church. His ministry is called EPIC (Experiential Participatory Interactive and Connecting with God). EPIC provides non-Eucharistic worship services for young adults. On Friday evenings, lay preachers and lay presiders offer worship services for young adults. This is not to diminish or minimize the importance of the Catholic Eucharist but rather to point toward it. The service invites young adults to the table, but it also acknowledges that some of them are not ready to be there yet. EPIC also offers a coffee house after each of these worship services on Friday evenings to gather folks for conversation and sharing. EPIC is expanding to offer evangelical-style missions and large group lectures on the essence of Catholic faith, and it is connecting also with seekers at local community colleges.

We want to create what we call a "relational net" in our parish that will touch all people, beginning first with our own baptized Catholics. Recent findings of the United States Census suggest that neighborhood or social contact between and among people in America today is dying and in certain areas is dead. We are a people who at times are pushing garage door openers and rolling into our condos and townhouses, and we do not even know our neighbors. We are retreating to channel surfing and playing with the computer rather than having relationships.

To address this growing disconnection between people, we are trying to break our parish up into twenty zones with close to three hundred neighborhood ministries. Unlike our small Christian communities, our twenty miniparishes are geographically determined. Neighborhood ministers, through visits, phone calls, socials, and home Masses, are the parish's presence in the grass roots. We hope to move much of the ministry out of the parish into the zones and into the small Christian communities to better connect with the many people we are not currently connecting with. This is not only for young adult Seekers, but for midlifers and seniors as well.

We emphasize more highly relational evangelizing in our parishes. There are some things we need to pay attention to, especially for the Catholic audience. We need to be doing year-round inquiry, year-round RCIA work for folks who are presenting themselves to us. They shouldn't have to wait until the next "cycle." We have got to get out of that fall-to-spring mentality. We also need to be engaged in efforts to be a reconciling parish. People have been hurt by the church, and we have to offer the process of healing and reconciliation.

Steven Ministries of St. Louis (www.stephenministries. com) is very effective in sensitizing a congregation for happenstance encounters with the un- or under-churched. This is where the Willow Creeks and the evangelical churches really have much to teach us; we need to benchmark them. They uncork the power of the ordinary person coming to church to be the evangelizer. In happenstance encounters, around the water cooler or the back fence for example, the invitation can be offered to "come to my church and discover some of what I have experienced."

We also make special efforts to reach Seekers who attend our weekend Masses. Our presiders try to be welcoming as we begin the liturgy. We have a welcoming of newcomers ministry where we ask all newcomers to stand, and we bless them as a congregation. We also have a breakfast after that gathering that begins a three-step process of welcoming. After this breakfast, newcomers are given a thorough explanation of the vision and ministries of the parish. Sometime later, they are visited in their homes by a neighborhood minister. Then quarterly, we meet them again for breakfast to see how they are doing.

As a community we all join hands at the Lord's Prayer as a sign of our connection and our solidarity. Welcoming Seekers is not just a Sunday-morning phenomenon—it is a throughout-the-week phenomenon. One of the struggles we have is to constantly remind our administrative staff that they are the front door people to the parish. If a person receives a bad response on a phone call, he or she will likely never call back or want to visit us again.

Two obstacles in Catholic ministries that must be addressed as the church reaches out to Seekers are closed communion and the issues of divorce and remarriage. We know at Holy Family that at times folks who are Seekers are attending our church and are probably coming up for communion. We do not know that they are not Catholic yet. In dealing with this, we hold to the vision of the RCIA: "To receive communion to share in communion, to share in communion is to be in communion with that church." So when we become aware of folks who are Seeking in our church and already receiving communion, we ask them to abstain and we ask them to join our RCIA process. Some at first are a little taken aback by that, but I think if it is said gently and if it is said well, we can help them understand what communion means in the church. It has been my experience that they embrace this as long as they don't feel like we are screening people taking communion or throwing them out for taking it.

The divorce issue is always a tough one. Going though an annulment process to receive communion again and to get one's marriages blessed in church is a struggle. We have a huge ministry to the divorced in our parish that tries to make them feel welcome and involved in our community. We have just started two ministries that are quite successful. The fact is that annulment is where the Catholic Church is right now if you want to be remarried. So we have started an annulment support ministry that is run by people who have gone though the annulment process. They partner with those who are in this pre-annulment stage. They meet with them and help them go though all those difficult documents that need to be filled out to get an annulment. Another process that has been started is called "To Trust Again," which is run by divorced and remarried parishioners trying to prepare divorced Catholics, annulled, for remarriage. We are trying to do the best we can to transform and make these welcoming evangelizing experiences.

I am passionate about utilizing the practice and discipline of the RCIA for sacramental preparation. What we have worked very hard on at Holy Family for the last six years—whether it is Baptism, First Eucharist, Confirmation, or matrimony—is for all sacramental catechesis to be family-focused and an RCIA-like journey. We "hub" these experiences into the Sunday Masses. Folks come early or stay after Mass for family-based catechesis.

Some of these folks do not even know they are Seekers. All they know is that they want their kids to have the sacrament because of grandma, grandpa, or some other member of the family. We need to use these opportunities in which people are seeking sacraments to transform the entire family into seeking conversion and seeking the Lord, to use these moments as opportunities for evangelization. We meet many young, nonpracticing potentially seeking people through the religious education of their children and through sacramental catechesis.

If a church really wants to reach Seekers, I cannot stress enough the importance of a communications ministry. We have a full-time director of communications at our parish whose mission is to reach beyond the walls of our parish to best connect with the unchurched and the potentially seeking. We have a radio program on several channels in Chicago that combines rock music with a reflection on next Sunday's gospel. We also videotape the radio show and play that on cable access on Tuesday afternoons. We have a taped TV Mass that plays at noon on Sunday in about sixty suburbs on the area and live radio mass at 7:30 on Sunday morning. We have purchased thirty-second spots at a very inexpensive rate on cable access and have done some commercials that play on A&E, MSNBC, and CNN addressing issues that Seekers are looking for, such as meaning, belonging, and healing. We then invite them to come to Holy Family. We mail our bulletin home once a month to the apparently unchurched on our books, those who are not contributing financially. We have a parish newspaper that circulates to about 60,000 that we have inserted into our regional edition of the *Chicago Tribune*. We are developing an Internet ministry and developing the possibility of "streaming" our liturgies and activities as the beginning of an Internet radio station (www.holyfamilyparish.org) that we are calling "The Stream."

For a summary of what we do, we use the seven steps of evangelism that Willow Creek teaches, which we have adapted for our parish:

1. You sitting in the pews are evangelizers. You know someone that is potentially a Seeker. Connect with them.

2. When it is appropriate, give witness to how Christ and church have changed your life.

3. Invite them to a weekend service, which we hope is filled with great drama, music, preaching, and invitations to conversion.

4. Invite them to a middle-of-the-week prayer and study.

5. Invite these new members into small Christian communities or small groups to feed them in an ongoing way.

6. Help them to discern their gifts of the Holy Spirit, so that they can become active and involved members of the church from the get-go, rather than becoming a name on a card or in a computer system.

7. Invite them into stewardship and tithing financially. Invite them to sharing the gifts of the Holy Spirit, sharing their material resources so that God's work can be continued in this faith community.

How to "Seekerize" Your Church

REVEREND BILL ELDER, pastor
MountainTop Community Church, Birmingham, AL

It all starts with valuing those we call "Seekers." We at MountainTop derive our approach to reaching Seekers right from Jesus' own life and words. Luke 15:1–2 describes a scene where tax collectors and sinners are gathering around Jesus, and the Pharisees and teachers of the law mutter, "The man welcomes sinners and eats with them." They might just as easily have said, "Jesus values people who are not religious at all." Today, we refer to those folks as Seekers or unchurched people. And even in the Bible belt where I live there are millions of them. So, if we want to reach them with the good news of Christ, we must begin by valuing them the way Jesus did.

I think the Seekers of Jesus' day must have been amazed when he, the Righteous One, the Holy One, said, referring to himself, "For the Son of Man came to seek and save those who are lost." That was shocking in itself because religious leaders in that day came to church to enjoy fellowship with the found rather than to seek and save the lost.

But Jesus was different. Could he be for real? They watched. They saw him investing his precious resources on their behalf. They saw him risk his very life for their sake. They saw him be rejected by the religious establishment because of them. He loved being with them, no matter what their background, no matter how little they knew or how much they had sinned. He went out on a limb to rescue them. And they finally saw it. He was for real. They responded and followed, and the church was born, full of Seekers. If we want to reach them, we will have to do the same thing.

Valuing Seekers does not happen by simply stating that you value them on brochures and cards. It does not happen by simply assuming it is true throughout your church. After all, churches should care about reaching lost people. Right? Seekers, I have found, are all from Missouri. They are all saying, "Show me." And to do that, you need a Seeker-valuing community and environment in place.

Seekers don't even know how to tell you how to value them. You have to think this through for them. The good news is that Seekers don't expect it. So, even little things can make a huge difference. Also, finding that kind of church is still rare. Most churches concentrate on growing the found rather than reaching the lost. So, if the word gets out that your church really means it when it comes to reaching people who don't go to church, when a Seeker does consider giving church a try, chances are your church will be high on the list.

The downside of being known as a Seeker-targeted church is you may take some criticism from the churched community. They may talk about you as being too simple, too shallow, maybe even soft-pedaling the Gospel. But the proof of any church is seen in the life-change, the spiritual growth of its people, and God honors and grows churches that care about reaching lost people.

You may not attract as many seasoned Christians as you would like, which means growing Seekers into full devotion to Christ is crucial. The good news is that when a Seeker really connects with Christ, spiritual growth can be rapid. The bad news is that unchurched habits do not die easily. Unchurched people can easily fall back into life as before. That's why assimilation and community and service are vital to their development.

That's also why it is imperative that when a Seeker responds to the call to faith he or she realizes that the response includes a life of obedience, that "follow through" is not an "add on" but at the very heart of the salvation experience. There must be no compromise at the point of understanding that receiving Christ means dying to self and taking up one's cross. Cheap grace and cheap decisions are cruel and evil deceptions and must never be used in reaching Seekers.

I want to suggest two things that have to be in place for a church to be able to reach Seekers: a set of understandings and a set of processes.

UNDERSTANDINGS

Vision

"Without a vision the people perish," and the church becomes amoebic and anemic. And not just any vision will do. If you want to reach Seekers, I suggest you have a vision that puts reaching them at the very forefront of your reason for being as a church. The definitive vision statement is obviously Matthew 28:18–20, the Great Commission. The first part of the commission is evangelism, and the second part is discipleship. Following this model, a vision should include both of those ingredients, and I believe that reaching Seekers requires that evangelism be stated first.

When I was at the beginning of my ministry, I thought it was the other way around—I thought as a pastor we should first grow them up and then send them out. Soon, however, I began to notice that the people rarely felt like they were "grown enough" to evangelize. I used to think it was because they were not studying hard enough or because I was not teaching hard enough, until the day I really looked at how Jesus did it. Then I saw we were not growing deep because we were not going wide. If you want a healthy and maturing transformational community, do not let them turn inward. Do not let them disguise the turning inward with the rational, "We just want to get deep first, pastor." As I read the Bible, I realized that evangelism must always be on the front burner because that's where Jesus put it. Very simply, God honors those who go. Oh sure, you can become a church that is a mile wide and an inch deep if you neglect the second half of the great commission. So, just don't do that. Don't compromise the Gospel in any way as you go. But if you neglect the going, the truth is you will be an inch wide and an inch deep, no matter how much you want to talk about depth. Disciples emerge on the go.

At MountainTop our vision is "to reach unchurched people and help them become fully devoted followers of Jesus and fully participating members of Christ's church." I believe that some version of this vision will be at the core of every real Seeker-targeted church.

Willow Creek Community Church has set the pace for Seeker-targeted churches. It has been tremendously helpful in our church's life. Although there are about a thousand churches that are part of the Willow

Creek Association, it is not a denomination. It is simply an assembly of churches that would like to learn how to reach Seekers better. Churches representing scores of different denominations are represented in the association, which offers a multitude of resources (www.willowcreek.org). Willow Creek's vision is "to turn irreligious people into fully devoted followers of Jesus."

Core Values

The second understanding is that a vision must have core values, non-negotiables, which support the vision. At MountainTop we have seven core values, and number one is "reaching out." It's amazing how when it comes time to consider decisions, at the very top will be the question, "Will it help us reach more Seekers?" Our Seeker service is given the Sunday morning spot. Our believer-targeted service happens on Wednesday. Given our druthers, we might want to flip-flop that schedule, but we know that reaching Seekers is the most important thing we are called to do, and chances are we will reach more of them on Sunday morning than on Wednesday night. Parking is an issue we are dealing with right now. We don't have enough, so we're asking our core people to park far away from our building so Seekers can have the easiest go of it. We know that their experience needs to be as hassle-free as possible if we are going to have a shot at stimulating a return visit. There are so many things churches can do, good things. Without a clear vision and a supporting set of values, churches can dilute their efforts and become mediocre at best. God deserves our best, and we have discovered that to reach Seekers we have to present our best. Vision and values are crucial to that objective.

Profile

The church needs to know whom it's reaching out to, so you need to construct a Seeker profile. We had to research to understand what our area's culture was, who the unchurched people around us are and what they value. We think of our church as a missionary community in the midst of about 100,000 people within 15 miles of our campus. If we are going to reach them we must understand their culture and be fluent in their language. What are their values? What are their assumptions? What are their realities? What are the problems that they are working with?

Our Seekers are primarily well-educated, middle management and above professional, affluent, not against God or religion, just not interested in church because they do not feel that they need it. What they need most is family time and relaxing time. Sports and clubs are their sources of community. Their kids competing in sports and education are high priorities. They are good people, good providers, family-focused, and good citizens. They simply do not know what they are missing. They have had some religious involvement in the past, probably as children, and they think that that makes them OK with God. Their name is on the roll of some church. They generally have no fear of hell, and they are satisfied with the way things are going. They have the resources to travel. With all of this, they never seem to get around to going to church, opting to relax, play golf, work in the yard, or go to the beach instead. They have a built-up resistance to making commitments.

At the same time, they are living life at a very shallow level. Their marriages have grown ordinary; their parenting has become frustrating. Many times they try to fix their kids with money and stuff and programs. Denial is the coping mechanism of choice, which is often supplemented with alcohol, "workaholism," and "playaholism." They settle for this because they do not know that there can be anything more. Boredom is a huge problem. Solitude is threatening. Internet porn is frequent, as are extramarital affairs. Climbing the affluent status pyramid is a popular goal of the unchurched. Anger is a huge issue in their homes, and they don't have the foggiest notion on how to handle it. Whatever will help their kids get ahead, they will do. They appreciate quality things and experiences.

Barriers

You need to understand the barriers that have to be overcome to get to your Seekers, as well as your competition for their time and involvement.

Seekers often have several preconceptions about church that make church an unappealing prospect. They think church is boring, irrelevant, depressing, sloppy, money grubbing, a waste of time, confusing, unfriendly, hypocritical, stuffy, a hassle, out of their comfort zones, behind the times, innocuous, insignificant, and pretentious. They feel like they will not fit in because they are sure they won't understand the language or the routine. These preconceived barriers have to be faced and overcome.

You also need to understand your competition. The competition is actually very simple and very amorphous, and very strong. It is by no means other churches. It is literally anything else that could occupy church time, such as watching TV, reading the newspaper, chilling out, and a whole host of recreational opportunities. It's whatever people select to help them get renewed so they can handle the workweek.

Consequently, Sunday morning church must be a place that both explodes their negative preconceptions about church and at the same time is able to compete with everything else that is out there during the Sunday morning time slot. Church has to provide benefits superior to those that come along with competing activities. And church cannot simply promise that and not deliver. If that happens, Seekers will just see the whole thing as fraudulent advertising that confirms their incipient negative stereotypes.

But these basic understandings of Seekers will amount to very little without an action plan. It would be like having a good course syllabus and never actually teaching the course. To put these ideals into action, a church must first be what we call "Seekerized." You can

"Seekerize" your church by first figuring out how Seekers might experience Sunday morning at your church from the moment they drive on to your property until the time they leave. Then, simply maximize the positives (whatever would make a Seeker feel comfortable and want to return) and work very hard to eradicate the negatives (whatever would turn a Seeker off or would discourage a return visit).

First impressions for Seekers are extremely important, especially because he or she is most likely "uptight" about the whole business of coming to church. Our welcoming begins in the parking lot, where they are met by a smiling, upbeat, servant-hearted, parking team member. We try not to be too pushy, but being in the South, people do not want to be ignored. We want them to be welcomed by no less than four different "smiling" people by the time they get to their seats. They want to be able to find their way around without asking. So signage is very important. Err on the side of too much than too little.

Seekers, like all of us, hunger for community, even though they often don't realize it. They want an extended family. Deep down people really seek not just a place they can go and be accepted, like the local pub or country club, they want a real bunch of friends who will accept and encourage and even confront with love when necessary. That kind of community is found nowhere else on the planet other than in a real church.

Seekers are looking for a place that is real, that has heart. Church should be a real community that does not feel like it is simply playing games or presenting entertainment, even though it utilizes all kinds of media to communicate the message. Sometimes churches like ours are criticized for being too much fun or feeling too much like entertainment. If you attended our church you would see that it is exciting. It is not boring. It is uplifting. But I think if you talked with our people you would soon see that beneath it all is something deadly serious. We know that people are perishing all around us, and if they do not get the message of Christ, they will miss out on both abundant life here and eternal life in heaven. We are passionate about doing whatever it takes to rescue perishing people.

Churches need culturally relevant communication to reach Seekers. This kind of communication begins with a church recognizing that people do not think like they used to years ago. The attention span of adults has also dropped, to brevity expressed in nanoseconds. Incorporating that into our church service means getting the message into their minds as quickly as we can and using every available approach to put it across, which has something to do with bells and whistles—technology. But you can do this even with little bells and little whistles. Don't try it without any. That's like trying to spell with half of the alphabet.

Always remember that communication takes place in far more ways than verbally. It takes place in the composite experience that they have at church. Everything needs to be communicating the same

Seeker-targeted language. The architecture, the dress, the ambiance, it's all a part. A church must effectively speak the Seekers' language.

Felt Needs

For a Seeker to bypass familiar patterns and give church a chance, and especially for a Seeker to decide to come back after one visit, he or she must be convinced that some help will be given in dealing with some crucial or difficult area of life. This is where "felt needs" come in. By discovering what those felt needs are and speaking directly to those needs, a church can demonstrate that it really cares about people and that God is a resource worth considering. This can open the door for the full message of Christ. Dealing with felt needs is often the first step in helping Seekers realize that there is so much more to life than they are experiencing and that they need the transformation that only a real relationship with God through Christ provides. Think about it. This is exactly how Jesus taught—from felt needs to depth. The masses were getting hungry— and he addressed that issue and then went on to talk about his being the bread of life. There was the man in the crowd who wanted Jesus to be an arbiter between him and his brother over an inheritance dispute, and Jesus tagged on to that exchange with a major teaching on greed. His disciples were concerned about how they were going to find their way after he left them to return to heaven; and that gave him a chance to point them to the much deeper issue of his being the axis of creation—the way, the truth, and the life. By helping Seekers deal with issues like handling anger or anxiety or broken relationships or debt (the list goes on and on), it is very easy to offer some excellent advice from scripture as to how to handle whatever the issue happens to be and then to move deeper to the more crucial issues that lie beneath the surface and the depth solution being a real and personal relationship with Christ. Felt needs must always be only the introduction, the open door to the real substance that lies within the God—honoring dialog.

One of the biggest felt needs that Seekers have is for community, and that's where our members come in. Our folks know that their job is to become a bridge into God's community for a Seeker. The church service promises to deal with real life issues, and our members commit to reaching out to their Seeker friends about the services and the help that is being offered. Their reaching out actually presents an entry into community. So when you have both community and helpful, creative, engaging communication aligned to reach out, it's a powerful combination, a deliberate partnership, a covenant between people who are involved in the church and Seekers.

In addition to the five understandings that need to be in place to be able to reach Seekers, there are a couple of very strategic processes that need to come on line as well.

PROCESSES

A Total Approach

Take your Seeker profile, the preconceptions you know Seekers will have and a sense of the competition you are facing for their Sunday morning time investment, and evaluate everything that Seekers will experience when they show up some Sunday morning. Start from the moment the Seekers drive onto your property. Move through the entire experience including the process for exiting the property. You're looking for positives and negatives.

Seekerizing is like renovating your church. Big things happen in paying attention to the little details. So much is communicated in nonverbal ways. Pay attention to such things as sufficient parking and good signage. Seekers don't like to feel lost, and they often don't want to have to ask someone for directions. The greeters are vital to the whole experience. They need to be friendly, helpful, but nonmanipulative. Restrooms need to be clean and easy to find. The nursery needs to be state-of-the-art as to cleanliness and security issues. And when Seekers leave they need to be able to get in their cars and exit quickly and easily. The hassle factor is huge. You can have a great service, but if the morning ended with sitting in traffic for ten minutes before being able to move, the next time that Seeker thinks about whether to go to church or just to stay home and do something else, the less hassle option wins 95 percent of the time. Do everything you can to get rid of the hassle. Believers will cut you a great deal of slack in that category; Seekers won't.

One more thing that's needed to "Seekerize" your church is heart. A Seeker will be most impressed with "heart"—the synergy of spiritual authenticity and passion. Slick, by-the-numbers, professional packaging doesn't wear very well. Sharpness will get their attention but realness and passion will attract their hearts and keep their attention piqued. You can't act real. You can only be real, and so as you give attention to really developing disciples who care about reaching lost people and who love what they are becoming in Christ, you are putting in place the solid foundation that will carry the day with Seekers. Don't neglect the depth of your congregation as you reach out widely.

"Churcherizing" Your Seekers

By this I mean developing a process by which a Seeker can move naturally and easily into the community and heart of your church. Jesus made it very clear that you don't just go and reach the lost sheep; you rescue them and bring them back to your community. That means there must be a discipleship path in place that can take someone through a commitment to Christ into full devotion and full participation in the body of Christ. This involves a path that leads through membership, spiritual maturity, small groups, serving, and reaching out to others. The real challenge is to keep that path clear and fresh. Follow up is difficult but crucial. If Seekers don't get assimilated they can easily revert back to old habits.

The real challenge in reaching Seekers, as you might expect, will be in your own heart as a church. Does your church have the passion for doing whatever it takes to reach perishing people? It's risky. It will cause you to change. To do this will push you way beyond your comfort zones. It's much easier not to do it, to concentrate instead on the growing found sheep than rescuing lost ones. Reaching Seekers is somewhat like walking on water. The storm was ferocious. Jesus was walking on the water. Peter decided he'd rather be in the storm with Jesus than "playing it safe" in the boat. So, in Matthew 14:28 we read that Peter called out to Jesus with the request that Jesus should command him to come to him. Peter had learned that the key to making the miracle journey with Jesus was to be found taking risks with Jesus in a spirit of obedience. So Peter says, "Tell me to come to You, Lord," which Jesus is thrilled to do. Jesus gives Peter the command, and Peter steps out, and it happens. He walks on water—until he takes his eyes off Jesus and focuses on the storm. Then he sinks, and Jesus has to rescue him.

No doubt about it. When churches are willing to obediently step out of the boat to reach Seekers, to join Jesus on his incredibly exciting journey, they walk on water—and it doesn't get any better than that this side of heaven.

Connecting
Postmoderns

WAREHOUSE 242 STAFF TEAM
Charlotte, NC

Our philosophy of small groups is simple. They are the only ministry and the only program our church has. We are not a church *with* small groups; we are a church *of* small groups.

Warehouse 242 is a generational church, a "postmodern" church, that targets people in their 20s and 30s. We are an Evangelical Presbyterian church, but we have found that the evangelical tradition that clearly demarcates the follower of Christ from the nonfollower of Christ usually doesn't resonate with postmodern people. Evangelicals always have been very entrepreneurial about methods and formulas that draw a line that one has to cross to become a Christian. With postmodern people, it is a lot messier than that.

What we know about postmodern people is that in general they are converted to community before they are converted to Christ. We find that people are getting involved in relationships and community and wrapped right into the mainstream of the life of our church, but they have never made a personal faith commitment to Christ. Often we hear people say things like: "I was skeptical about the gospel and the Christian faith. All of a sudden, I woke up one morning after hanging out with these people and sharing life with them and realized that I believe this stuff. I don't know if I bought it yesterday, but I believe it today."

We are doing everything that we can within our tradition to break down the barriers between Christians and non-Christians, to be inclusive, and to not point fingers. Our mission statement is "connecting people to real relationships with God, each other, and the rest of the world." We exist for mission. There are around seven hundred churches in Charlotte. We started this church three years ago. Charlotte does not need another church. Many of them are half-empty. There is, however, a need for a church that says, "We are here to engage and connect people who are not yet connected to Christ."

What we have experienced in that short period of time is that people readily come to the gospel and to a personal faith commitment to Christ not through formally "joining" a church, but rather though the experience of community. A writer once said, "The best apologetic that Christians have in the postmodern era is the embodied apologetic of community." We want community to *be* evangelism, to have small groups that include both Christians and non-Christians.

We get a lot of questions about that philosophy, people saying, "Wait a minute—we've heard of Bible study groups and we've heard of evangelistic small groups, but to blend these two things together as your bread and butter, are you sure you want to do this?" And then they ask, "Isn't that really hard?" Yes, it really is, but we believe that is the way that the Christian life is meant to be lived—for Christians and non-Christians to rub shoulders together and to share life together moving toward Christ. This is the most effective evangelism for postmodern people.

We call our small groups, which are co-ed groups of ten to twelve people, C.pax. The letter "C" stands for "community"; and "pax" is designed to evoke two images: a pack, or group of people moving through life together, and *pax,* which is Latin for peace. We don't divide them by marital status or stage in life. They meet weekly in homes. They pray together, study scripture together, and oftentimes answer prewritten questions about last Sunday's sermon

But we also ask them to schedule weeks when the group goes bowling together or gets ice cream together—time where they can build relationships and that will be nonthreatening to non-Christians. We want them involved in service projects together and eating together. We want them passionately committed to reaching people who have not yet made a faith commitment to Christ.

We tell people that they will not enjoy life at Warehouse without being involved in a C.pak. We tell them without apology that if they come to Warehouse 242 and enjoy what we're doing here, that's great, but there are way too many people here on Sunday morning for them to get to know anyone. Spiritual life and growth and relationships happen in small groups. In fact, we don't even do announcements in church—all of that happens in small groups.

We've built our idea of these groups from Acts 2:42–47, where the 242 in our name comes from. The image in this passage is of people living and worshiping and eating and sharing communion in homes day to day. The gathering in the temple focused on worship; the real life of the church took place in homes. If there is a distinctive that Warehouse has, it is that we want our small groups, like the first churches described in Acts, to be fully functional.

To be honest, though, while our biggest area of emphasis is small groups, this is also one of our biggest weaknesses. We just have not hit our stride here yet. Part of that is that our leadership from the staff level has not been what it should have been. We have tended to be reactive, have not given our leaders the care they have needed, and have been too quick to appoint others to positions of leadership, and I am confident this will change.

One of our biggest ongoing emphases has got to be leadership training for C.pak leaders. The first area of leadership training is mission, where we say to our people, "We are here to love this culture and the people in the culture that Christ loved." We are not scared of it in our worship or our life together; we do not want to make the same mistakes that Christians have often made, such as speaking at the culture rather than to it, of setting up an us-versus-them dynamic, where we portray the culture and the people as somehow enemies

Second, we do everything that we can to help our C.pak leaders understand how to build a biblically functioning community, which can be a challenge when you have a group with both intense followers of Christ and others who are not. They also face difficulties bridging the sometimes-wide gaps in age and life experience between the group members. We spend a lot of time looking at what biblical community is and helping them understand how to develop it.

Core to us, as in the Celtic tradition, is developing ministry. We don't want anyone to sit on the benches at Warehouse. We believe that we need every single person understanding and functioning in his or her spiritual gifts and living out the mission of the gospel and the mission that God has given us. We help our C.pak leaders understand how to involve everyone and show that everyone brings something to the table, as well as how to experience this together in community.

A postmodern community is like a potluck: No one really knows what else someone is going to bring, but because everyone is there together, everyone has brought something. That is the way the postmodern people experience life, church, and community in small groups together—we emphasize involving everyone.

The last element we emphasize is a holistic spirituality. Many times, people keep church separate from their real lives—it's just something they do on Sunday morning or Wednesday night, and in the rest of their lives they work, raise children, figure out a way to pay the bills, mow the lawn, take vacations, and jog. Christianity is important to them, but they keep it to the side.

We have learned many lessons from the Celtic Christians who had prayers for everything from tucking their children into bed at night to tamping down the fire to men splashing water on their faces three times to remind themselves that God exists in trinity. We do everything that we can to help our folks understand that spirituality should pervade all of life, when we rise in the morning, when we drink coffee, when we sip wine, when we eat, when we make love, and when we work. Everything we do ought to be seen as an act of devotion and an act of worship. We want our C.pax to live life together in that model, where Christianity is not a discrete activity from the rest of life, but an experience of community that fuels the rest of life.

People get involved in C.pax because that's all we have to involve them in—that makes it easy. Every Sunday we put cards on the chairs for people to fill out if they want to join a C.pak, and we have a C.pax information table outside the meeting room. The groups keep growing because people in C.pax invite their friends. This works because people won't make the commitment to be involved in C.pax and in the life of a small group if tons of other things are competing for their time and attention.

The very first Sunday that Warehouse 242 met in the fall of 1999, we said from the stage: "Look, for those of you who are followers of Christ, we have a basic conviction that Christians go to church way too much. If we were to offer you an activity for every night of the week, you would be there. We could fill up your time with endless church activities. The only problem with that is that it is keeping us from interacting and living life with the very people that Christ interacted and lived life with—the very people that we are called together to reach."

We told them we want them to worship, but other than that we did not want to see them. We want our people to be involved in C.pax, to live spiritual lives in ministry as commissioned missionaries from Warehouse 242 to the culture—in fact, it is our hope that more people will be involved in C.pax than attend worship.

We are still learning about small groups and community, and right now we are wrestling with two big issues that we still don't have definitive answers for. One is do we need more diversity or more affinity in our C.pax? We have been intent about holding to our belief that we want to throw everyone—single, married, young, old—everyone together in one big pot because that is what biblical experience is supposed to be. In a lot of cases, the results of such mixing has been amazing, such as the 56-year-old developer mentoring the 18 year old who is trying to figure out his life. That intergenerational piece of the ministry has been wonderful.

But at the same time we are beginning to hear from our folks that there are times in their lives when they really need to be around a group of people who are going though the same thing that they are. So we are launching some C.pax for newly married couples, and this is causing us to question our core philosophy, which is good. We do not mind questioning our core philosophy and shaking things up—change is also one of our core values. The end is to get people involved in community, and the means is C.pax. We will switch up what ever needs to be switched up to see that happen.

The second thing that we are learning and really struggling with now is how we can make C.pax leadership sustainable for people over the long haul. In no uncertain terms, C.pax leaders are the pastors of our church, not the professional religious people on our staff. They are on the front lines; they are caring for people, which is exhausting when you have another job and another life. We are asking how we as the leaders of the church can encourage, mentor, and give these folks the resources that they need so that C.pax ministry will last over time.

All of our leaders now are identifying and developing apprentice leaders who can lead groups that form from the original groups. How can we ensure that a leader does not get to the point where they let the apprentice take over the group? How can we make sure that the ministry is sustainable and that the apprentice goes on to lead a new group? We are in the middle of trying to figure that out.

✦

The Power of Commitment:

IT CAN HAPPEN ANYWHERE

✦

MARJORY ZOET BANKSON, steward
Seekers Church, Washington, DC

The question is often asked, "How can a tiny church accomplish so much?" And our answer is that we can do this "stuff" *because* we are a tiny church with a culture of call and commitment.

The Seekers Church in Washington, DC, has about seventy-five adults, fifteen children, and no single pastor, though we do have a part-time paid leadership team. We are an offspring of Church of the Saviour, which was founded by Gordon and Mary Cosby right after World War II on the basis of small, highly committed mission groups. We are not interested in a bigger church or a lot of programs. Focus and intentional service are what we want to foster.

We assume that Jesus has a call for every person, not just for clergy, not just for seminarians, but also for everyone. We believe that when people begin to look at their own lives and ask where God is calling them to ministry, enormous change can happen, both for themselves and their communities. Every person who comes to the church is soon invited to think about what his or her call is and how Seekers can support that.

ROOTS

The Seekers Church was started about twenty-five years ago, just weeks before my husband and I arrived in Washington, DC. We had been reading books about Church of the Saviour by Elizabeth O'Connor with titles such as *Call to Commitment* (HarperCollins), *Journey Inward, Journey Outward* (HarperCollins), and *Eighth Day of Creation* (W Publishing Group), and we looked forward to being in a church that took discipleship seriously. Instead we found a chaotic mix of newly forming communities, each with a distinct mission and a small core of committed members.

About a year before we arrived, Gordon Cosby had come to the conclusion that Church of the Saviour had gotten too big (at 120 members), and that he was not called to administer so many different ministries. A task force was formed to listen for God's leading, and after much prayer and study of biblical precedents they "heard" a call to "cross the Jordan" and claim separate "lands." The New Lands proposal birthed six little churches in the spring and summer of 1976. Later, four more developed and one died, but when we arrived everyone was anxious about which key people would join each small church. Peter and I were afraid we had arrived at a funeral.

Instead, however, we discovered it was a time of real creativity and new life. We stepped into the opening scene of another cycle in the life of Church of the Saviour, which had always valued the fluidity and changing nature of God's call over preservation of institutional structures. Spreading the leadership among six little churches meant there was more space for emerging gifts in all of them. For those who still wanted Gordon's vision and inspiration, there was a weekly ecumenical worship service in the headquarters building, but belonging, decision-making, and financial responsibility happened in each little church.

SEEKERS

Today, the word "Seeker" is being used as a term for people who are basically unchurched and looking for a home or those who might wander in without any sense of commitment, but that is not our charism. When Seekers Church was formed in 1976, we found inspiration in a book by Robert Greenleaf titled *Servant Leadership* (Paulist Press). Greenleaf says: "Prophets occur in every generation. It is the quality of listening that calls forth prophets. It is Seekers then who make prophets in our midst." We choose to name ourselves Seekers Church because we wanted to be those deep listeners to one another. We wanted to be a place where prophetic alternatives could be nurtured.

Robert Greenleaf was an executive with AT&T, and he brought a fresh perspective to understanding dispersed leadership. He described leaders who did not act like autocrats or celebrities, but who took the servant role of Jesus as a guide that would evoke caring among employees and customers too. Greenleaf's work spoke deeply to Fred Taylor and Sonya Dyer, who were engaged in a mission of Church of the Saviour called FLOC (For Love of Children). Fred and Sonya were ready to offer their leadership to start Seekers, and they wrote the initial call of Seekers to support ministry by every member.

Each of the sister communities birthed by Church of the Saviour in 1976 was formed around a call that gave it a particular identity. Healthcare, housing, intercultural education, job placement, and refugee assistance were some of the defining missions. Seekers Church claimed God's call on our lives in the ordinary structures of our lives (home, work, primary relationships, and citizenship) as the core value to be nurtured and invigorated by creative worship. Because of our roots in FLOC, many Seekers are involved in some form of child advocacy in Washington, DC, or abroad, but the center of our life together is dynamic worship with seasonal liturgies rather than a single mission.

Visitors find us on the web (www.seekerschurch.org) or because they have read about Church of the Saviour and are looking for a church in that tradition that specifically values children. In worship, they see handmade bulletin covers, provocative liturgy, and thematic altars. Sometimes a child offers the "word for children." Each week a different person—usually from the congregation—preaches. Sermons can be personal testimony, theological reflection, or community guidance and are available on the web so people who are away can engage in the conversations initiated by these sermons. We do follow the common lectionary, and continuity is maintained by a liturgist from the Celebration Circle mission group, but each week is something of an adventure for all of us.

ONGOING FORMATION

After attending worship or perhaps a family overnight, we encourage people to attend our School of Christian Living on Tuesday nights. Because preaching comes from many different perspectives and thus does not provide the consistent educational focus of a single preacher, the central teaching function at Seekers is held by the Learners & Teachers mission group. I belong to L&T because I am drawn by my own call to outreach teaching and because I believe that ongoing education is critical for developing a community of conscious people who want to embody God's call in the world.

Part of the work of L&T is to discern what the growing edge of our congregation really is. What is the Holy Spirit doing in the congregation? How do we need to undergird ministry? Deepen our spiritual life? Encourage disciplines? What classes are needed now? Our authority in the wider community comes from doing that work consistently and self-critically over time.

Classes in the school focus on both content and accountability. Teachers are encouraged to make the classes relational to encourage personal application of the concepts and ideas encountered. Assignments introduce the practice of written reflection, something we expect and encourage as an ongoing practice. L&T does not just take anyone who volunteers to teach, although we do take any offer as an indication that call may be stirring in that person. The school is a place for people to exercise emerging gifts or interests and perhaps teach with a mentor as a way of developing new leadership. Since our mission is both to initiate classes and to oversee them, we also provide a shepherd in each class to pray for each member and follow up with those who miss class. That way accountability and commitment are encouraged from the beginning.

We do emphasize the theme of call in many classes, so newcomers become acquainted with our culture of call, gifts, ministry, and reflection—the journey inward and the journey outward. In each term, we offer a biblical class and one or two other classes—spiritual growth, Christian doctrine, incubating mission, or some creative expression like dance, quilting, or clowning. The school meets on Tuesday evenings, and we provide a simple meal so that people can come right from work, eat together, have a short meditation to help with transition from the workday, and then go to the ninety-minute classes. We expect participants to do assignments and come regularly for the twelve-week term.

That's the first resistance we run into. Attending regularly for twelve weeks seems too long and difficult with all the other obligations that people have. We ask people to just try it, as this is a taste of intentional community. Purposely putting ourselves in a situation that will surely take us, student and teacher alike, beyond our comfort zone is valued as a way of opening ourselves to God's call to challenge unconscious or exploitive cultural patterns. We have learned that people can usually commit to six weeks at a time, so recently we've tried offering two six-week installments instead of one twelve-week class. There has been some shifting in and out at the six-week point and the sense of community is definitely disrupted, but we've discovered that we may have more flexibility than we thought.

In the summer, we usually have one class, shorter terms (three to four weeks), and a brown-bag supper to accommodate travel and vacations. No matter what the season though, we typically have twenty to twenty-five people at the school. That's 30 percent of the congregation!

MISSION GROUPS

The primary structure for spiritual formation at Seekers is commitment to a mission group. We ask people to attend at least two twelve-week sessions in the School of Christian Living before joining a mission group so they have a chance to explore their own call and feel the power of community with a common purpose. After two classes in the school, people can move into a mission group.

A mission group typically has six or eight people who share a common intention for the work described in its call. We've found that if people get into a small group with no specific call, then differences or disagreements can cause the group to founder. Sharing a larger purpose can create space and a reason to work out those differences, although it takes both skill and spiritual maturity to handle conflict in a way that produces growth rather than resentment. It's a bit like being married to the mission!

For the past eighteen years, I have been in Learners & Teachers because that's my call and ministry. I had a teaching background as a high school history teacher, but when I started to teach classes at the School of Christian Living I felt free to combine my interest in biblical studies with creative methods I'd developed in the classroom. Later I decided that I wanted more theological education because of the questions that my mission group kept raising about my call, so I eventually went to seminary. In 1985, I was hired as the first female president of Faith@Work, a relational and ecumenical national ministry. After all these years of speaking to conferences, editing a magazine, and leading retreats for F@W, I still teach classes regularly at Seekers and coach younger teachers in how to combine theological depth and relational methods. Those weekly meetings of the mission group sustain me in lean times and challenge me in fat years.

In the mission group, we see long-term spiritual formation taking place through the combination of inward and outward practices. In Learners & Teachers, I have a spiritual director, and every week I give her a written report that describes where God is at work in my inward life (prayer, study, dreams, nagging images); my outward journey (work, volunteer efforts, money); and in the community (relationships, initiative, disagreements). She looks for themes over time, asks questions, and sometimes makes suggestions. Her role is to help me see the presence of God and God's call in my daily life. I have stayed in the same mission group even though everyone else has shifted in or out because my call to "outreach teaching" has continued to expand and the group gives me a place to pastor—and receive that from others. I am often gone on the weekends, but I am always at my mission group meeting on Tuesday night because that is my place of accountability, grounding, and growth in the community.

New mission groups are formed when two or three members of Seekers prayerfully discern a particular service they want to offer. A written call is then "sounded" in the congregation and the group develops a common practice (or regular spiritual discipline), which they agree to share. The group meets regularly to pray, share their emerging vision, and discern the gifts they have in the group to carry out this particular mission. At a minimum, each group needs a "pastor-prophet" to hold the call up regularly and a spiritual guide to encourage spiritual development by responding to weekly written reports and asking questions that may clarify the Spirit's internal work. As specific actions become clear, the group begins to carry out its mission as a "body of Christ." The work of each mission group is largely independent of outside supervision and therefore carries considerable responsibility for its internal health and external activities, including financial obligations. Because of the commitment involved, people usually belong to only one group.

WORK OF MINISTRY

Living as a congregation of mission groups has changed the way that we worship and run our church.

We do not have a paid pastor, though we do have a part-time paid staff whose primary job is discernment and coordination, and we keep all members up-to-date through our detailed web site.

Decisions involving the whole church are made by a core group of twenty-four Stewards. In order to encourage accountability to the larger body of the church, each mission group must have at least two Stewards—experienced members who have made a public commitment to care for the whole congregation rather than just one of the mission groups. That circle of Stewards is open to anyone who is willing to make the extra commitment of time, energy, money, and accountability to care for the whole.

The Stewards meet monthly and speak from where they are located in a mission group, so they serve as a representative body in that sense. The agenda for Stewards' meeting is prepared by the three-member staff team (who are also Stewards). The staff team has no particularly visible role, but they watch for issues or needs in the community that are not currently being handled by mission groups, and we have acknowledged the importance of their leadership and discernment function with a stipend. Currently there are no other paid functions.

My husband, Peter, is on the staff team with two women from the congregation. He lives out the external call of Seekers Church through his work at Communities-in-Schools (CIS), a faith-based organization that has been working to keep marginal children in school for more than thirty years. He is in the national office, making links between local programs and government funding. CIS is a place where he can talk about how God is moving in his life and where people are willing to listen and share their own stories as part of their work environment. Now Peter is working there three days a week to free up time for Seekers, and CIS has been willing to support that too.

Living out of call means connecting the different parts of our lives—work, play, and worship. Peter is in Celebration Circle, the mission group that supports our worship life. He's been named the "imagineer" because of his creative ideas for liturgy and the altar. Also, when a woman preaches, Peter is the regular male liturgist. He "holds the silence" during extended prayer times in worship, and his experience anchors the creativity that comes with different preaching every week. For both of us, weekly mission group meetings keep us grounded in this particular body of Christ, but meeting for worship is an important way for the whole community to celebrate God's presence in our midst.

All Stewards are expected to be in a mission group, but other members of Seekers are free to live out their accountability relationships in a variety of ways. Some meet one-to-one with a spiritual director. Others join a task force without the spiritual disciplines of a mission group for some particular short-term purpose. Others sample community in their classes at the School of Christian Living.

To deepen the inner life of the whole community, there is a monthly gathering of Spiritual Guides that is open to anyone who wants to grow in that direction. Because all the guides have been chosen by consensus in their mission groups, they hold the stories shared in spiritual reports and embody a good deal of trust. The Spiritual Guides function as a peer group around different monthly topics such as developing new leaders for silent retreats, deepening the spiritual life of Stewards, and "What is the difference between therapy and spiritual direction?" Some of the guides also have accountability relationships with people who do not belong to a mission group but nevertheless want to grow in their ability to reflect on where call is taking them.

WORSHIP

Worship is the place where we all come together. We use the common lectionary because we want to remember that we are part of the wider church of Jesus Christ. We are not just a handmade church doing whatever we feel like doing. We ask that each person who is preaching be attentive to the lectionary scripture and to speak for fifteen minutes so that we have time for reflections from the congregation. Because everyone has been working with the same scriptures during the week, sometimes the response simply highlights another part of the readings than one that the preacher used. Sometimes we take issue with the preacher's interpretation, but more often the response affirms and perhaps extends what the preacher has offered.

Although we have a number of people who have been through seminary, that is not a prerequisite for preaching at Seekers. Celebration Circle does look for a sense of God's revelation in those who volunteer to preach, but it does not seek to control the content (though guidelines and coaching are available). It is a powerful experience to speak from experience, relating it to scripture. Quite often, after people have preached two or three times, they began to say, "Hmmm, I want to do more with Bible study." A number of our people have gone to seminary after preaching or teaching at Seekers. We are fortunate that there are several seminaries nearby where people can take classes.

Our commitment to seeking and living out God's call also requires that we be committed to failure. If we did not feel free to fail, we would not feel free to take risks on a lot of things we do. Our church structure does not have in place someone wagging his or her finger at us if it doesn't come out like we originally intended or if we do not reach the goals we set for ourselves. This freedom has allowed us tremendous learning. Frankly, a lot of times someone will start with a really good idea and a sense of a call from God, but once she is in the middle of it, things change, heading off in directions we never imagined. Then we just have to just let go! It is important for us to let go of things that no longer have the breath of life in them so that we are not always spending energy trying to keep things alive when God is moving elsewhere. We need that kind of energy to take on the things that really work.

One example of this emerging direction of call is that for twenty-five years we thought we needed a choir. We wanted a choir. We had a monthly "sing-along," but no one felt called to initiate a choir. Then a group formed to offer music in worship—choose hymns, provide some live music, and choose a recorded prelude. The group struggled with the requirements of being a mission group (particularly the accountability of regular attendance and doing spiritual reports). They struggled with what it means to work with their musical gifts and what that means to be offering their gifts to God. This is taking them into a very different set of understandings than just being a church choir. It's going to be interesting to see how this comes out.

Another way that Seekers supports living out of call is the Growing Edge Fund. Anyone can submit a proposal to the three voluntary directors. It's designed to give people money to explore something or try something out that may or may no be a calling. This often-times results in far-reaching evangelism work. We recently gave money to a young woman to develop some of her photographic talents and abilities. Cynthia has a passion for understanding what God is doing with women working the land in the Midwest. She has done some wonderful photo essays that explain their commitment to sustainable agriculture, and we are glad to be a part of her effort. She has put her roots down spiritually with us, but she is gone a lot. She makes a little money for herself doing dental hygiene, and then she is off on another photographic project in some distant place. Two or three of us stay in touch on a regular basis, and we celebrate when she comes home. This is just one example of a person who was called to a prophetic ministry by Seekers.

Almost everyone in our congregation has a story like Cynthia's. We have a young man who quit his job with a large shipping firm and is now doing quite well running a foundation that provides inoculations to children in Russia. Things like that come out of call. We do not have to plan. We believe that if we hold each other accountable to keep pressing the edges so that God's love can show through our transparencies, we will attend to the lost, the least, and the lonely ones that Jesus included at God's banquet table.

BIBLICAL MODEL

Seekers Church is a place of constant formation. Recently I felt led to release my full-time position with Faith@Work so a younger person could step in. Now my mission group is asking, "Where are you being called?" Because of what I understand of God's claim on our lives, I trust that some new call will develop. Right now I'm still writing and speaking, but

I don't have to be responsible for the ministry of F@W. I am here to listen for God's next call, and the mission group structure helps me do that.

This model of committing to seeking and living out God's call is actually a very old biblical model. Jesus called twelve very unlikely, ordinary men. We know there were women who traveled with them as well. Jesus invited them to make a commitment to God and to each other for those at the margins of society. That call, and their willingness to be shaped by it, is still changing the world.

At Seekers, we take the invitation to answer God's call seriously, and we know that empowers people to be the hands and feet of Christ in the world. This is the model we live from. It is a model that will work in any church but you have to create a climate for it, where everybody must be encouraged to think in terms of call. It can happen anywhere.

Presenters

Reverend Duane Arledge is the minister of missions at Riverside Baptist Church in Denver. He oversees an exciting church planting program that has birthed more than twenty churches, including ministries to Hispanic, Indonesian, Japanese, and biker congregations. He currently also is serving as interim pastor of a new Riverside church plant in South Denver.

REVEREND DUANE ARLEDGE
darledge@riversidebaptist.com
Riverside Baptist Church
2401 Alcott Street   (303) 433-8665
Denver, CO 80211   www.riversidebaptist.com

Marjory Zoet Bankson is the former editor of *Faith@Work* magazine. Bankson is a regular preacher and teacher at Seekers Church, an innovative worshipping community of Church of the Saviour in Washington, DC. She travels and speaks extensively about lay involvement in churches.

MARJORY BANKSON
MZBankson@aol.com
Seekers Church
276 Carroll Street NW   (202) 829-9882
Washington, DC 20012   www.seekerschurch.org

Monsignor Arturo Bañuelas is the pastor of St. Pius X in El Paso, TX, a dynamic congregation that blends Latino spirituality with Vatican II consciousness. The author of *Mestizo Christianity,* Father Bañuelas is also the founder of the Tepeyac Institute at St. Pius X, which educates thousands of lay leaders annually.

FATHER ARTURO BAÑUELAS
hopie12@aol.com
St. Pius X
1050 North Clark   (915) 772-3226
El Paso, TX 79905   www.elpasodiocese.org/tei

Reverend Mark Beckwith is the rector of All Saints Episcopal Church in Worcester, MA, established in 1835. Its current congregation of six hundred is involved in ecumenical feeding programs and is a participant in the Interfaith Hospitality Network, providing housing for homeless families. The church actively reaches into the changing neighborhood that surrounds it.

REVEREND MARK BECKWITH
Mbeckwith@allsaintschurchworc.org
All Saints Episcopal Church
10 Irving Street   (508) 752-3766
Worcester, MA 01609   www.allsaintschurchworc.org

Father Patrick Brennan, the only full-time, resident priest at the 10,000-member Holy Family Parish in a Chicago suburb, keeps this Catholic variation on the Willow Creek megachurch manageable through extensive lay participation. Father Brennan is also the author of several books on evangelism.

FATHER PATRICK BRENNAN
fr.pbrennan@holyfamilyparish.org
Holy Family Parish
2515 Palatine Road   (847) 359-0042
Inverness, IL 60067   www.holyfamilyparish.org

Valerie Chapman, a Catholic laywoman, is a pastoral administrator at St. Francis of Assisi in Portland, OR. Fueled by a passion for social justice, the parish lives the "messy word" of the Gospel with a dining hall for the homeless and multiple services for the poor.

VALERIE CHAPMAN
vorazio@mail.ptld.uswest.net
St. Francis of Assisi
330 SE 11th Avenue
Portland, OR 97214   (503) 232-5880

Father Donald Cozzens, former rector of St. Mary Seminary in Cleveland, is also a professor of pastoral theology and author of the acclaimed *The Changing Face of the Priesthood.* An experienced counselor, he has guided many lay people and clergy in ministry.

FATHER DONALD COZZENS
dcozzens@jcu.edu
John Carroll University
Department of Religious Studies
University Heights, OH 44118   (216) 397-1731

Father Walter Cuenin, pastor of Our Lady Help of Christians in Newton, MA, cooperates with a large lay staff to serve this 2,600 family parish in suburban Boston. He is one of the organizers of the Priests Forum in Boston.

FATHER WALTER CUENIN
whcuenin@ourladys.com
Our Lady Help of Christians
573 Washington Street   (617) 527-7560
Newton, MA 02458   www.ourladys.com

Reverend Gary Davis is the founding pastor of Church in the Wind, a congregation for bikers that is a church plant of Riverside Baptist Church in Denver, and a coordinator of the nationwide Church in the Wind church plant program.

REVEREND GARY DAVIS
citw@churchinthewind.org
Church in the Wind
PO Box 211277   (303) 427-1538
Denver, CO 80221   www.churchinthewind.org

Reverend Bill Elder is the pastor of MountainTop Community Church in Birmingham, AL. This Willow-Creek style, Seeker-sensitive church has grown from a group of 10 meeting in Reverend Elder's living room to a congregation of more than 1,500.

REVEREND BILL ELDER
pastor@mountaintopchurch.com
MountainTop Community Church
1001 Vestavia Parkway   (205) 823-7090
Birmingham, AL 35216   www.mountaintopchurch.com

Reverend Patricia Farris, the first female senior pastor of First United Methodist Church in Santa Monica, CA, gave new life to this century-old church by instituting lay-driven leadership and mentoring potential leaders through small groups.

REVEREND PATRICIA FARRIS
revfarris@aol.com
First United Methodist Church
1008 11th Street   (310) 393-8258
Santa Monica, CA 90403   www.santamonicaumc.org

Reverend Bill Geis's innovative work of applying "partnering" concepts from the business world to his ministry in rural Southwest Oklahoma has given life not only to the three Lutheran congregations he oversees, but also to the surrounding communities.

REVEREND BILL GEIS
WSgeis@lutheranOK.com
Lutheran Ministries of Southwest Oklahoma
PO Box 368   (580) 846-5459
Lone Wolf, OK 73655   www.lutheranok.com

Dawn Mayer is a pastoral associate and director of family faith and life at Holy Family Parish in Inverness, IL, and Church of the Holy Spirit in Schaumburg, IL.

DAWN MAYER
dmayer@holyfamilyparish.org
Holy Family Parish
2515 Palatine Road   (847) 359-0042
Inverness, IL 60067   www.holyfamilyparish.org

Father Thomas McGread is a retired pastor of St. Francis of Assisi in Wichita, KS. By teaching stewardship of time and talent, before treasure is asked for, he turned his congregation into one that joyfully gives. His model has been used throughout the country.

FATHER THOMAS McGREAD
6900 E. 45th Street North
Wichita, KS 67212   (316) 744-0853

Sister Clara Stang, O.S.F., who has a background in community organizing for the poor, is the vice president and assistant minister for the Franciscan community of Little Falls, MN. She previously served for eight years on a team of three nuns and two priests who ministered to five small rural parishes in Western Minnesota.

SISTER CLARA STANG
stangosf@info-link.net
Franciscan Sisters of Little Falls
116 8th Avenue SE   (320) 632-2981
Little Falls, MN 56345   www.fslf.org

Warehouse 242 in Charlotte, NC, is a cutting-edge, Generation-X focused church that ministers to a unique congregation of more than five hundred members, most of them in their 20s.

WAREHOUSE 242
info@warehouse242.org
1213 C West Morehead Street   (704) 344-9242
Charlotte, NC 28208   www.warehouse242.org